THE SECRET OF TATE'S BEACH

By Augusta Huiell Seaman

Cover illustration by Tanya Glebova
Cover design by Robin Fight
© 2022 Jenny Phillips
goodandbeautiful.com

Originally published in 1926

CONTENTS

    I. The Lonely Beach 1
   II. At the Foot of the Figurehead 11
  III. The Mystery of Peggy 22
  IV. Peggy Changes Her Mind 33
   V. In Which Peggy Redeems Her Promise 45
  VI. The Heart of the Mystery 54
 VII. Old Captain Wareham 62
VIII. The Number Three Surfman 71
  IX. What Old Dr. Trenway Remembered 84
   X. On the Trail of Jonas Tow 96
  XI. A Clue at Last 106
 XII. A New Factor 112
XIII. Dr. Scott Takes a Hand 122
XIV. The First Results 132
 XV. Several New Developments 141
XVI. A Meddler in the Mystery 150
XVII. Crab Meat and Consequences 158
XVIII. Peggy Makes a New Concession 167
XIX. The Captain Joins the Trio 176
 XX. The Night of the Storm 185
XXI. Peggy Learns the Truth 194
XXII. The Doctor Has an Inspiration 202
XXIII. The Answer to the Riddle 209

CHAPTER I

The Lonely Beach

A LONG, LEVEL LINE of surf fretting the coast as far as the eye could see. Back of the beach the dunes, shaggy, irregular, odorous of glossy bay and rank seagrass. Nestling behind one of the highest dunes, sheltered from the east winds, one low, rambling two-storied house, gray, weatherworn, innocent of paint. A wide veranda, closed in by rusty screening, encircled the building. There was no other human habitation in sight, all up and down the fifteen miles of coast, except the towering shaft of Barnegat Light in the distance and the near bulk of a Coast Guard station half a mile to the north.

This was the scene that met the gaze of Merwin Scott as she clambered to the top of a dune and stood there contemplating the wide expanse of gray-green ocean before her and the wilderness of sand and sea-grass all about. A stiff northeast wind whipped her scarf about her and wafted salt spray to her lips. Low, gray clouds raced across the sky, and one solitary coastwise steamer edged along the horizon, leaving a trail of smoke behind.

"Like it, honey?"

She started at the unexpected sound of a voice and wheeled to face the tall, spare form of a man who had come up behind her. Then she slipped an arm through his and looked up seriously into the kindly brown eyes looking down at her.

"I don't just know, Daddy. It's . . . it's awfully wild and lonely, isn't it? I'd have to get used to it before I really know whether I like it or not."

"You'll have ample time to get used to it before we're through, and then you'll *love* it—or I miss my guess!"

"Well, if I can learn to feel about it the way you do, I'm sure I'll love it," Merwin acknowledged, giving her father's arm a little squeeze. "And I hope I shall," she added, "especially if it's got to be my home for so long. How long must it be, Dad? Not very long, I hope."

She looked at him wistfully, and he suppressed a sigh as he answered with forced cheerfulness:

"Not more than a few months, I'm quite certain. Pneumonia left you so thoroughly run down, you know, and your summer in the mountains has done you no good. Now we'll try this wonderful sea air and life for a while, and you must live out of doors absolutely all the time except when you're in to eat and sleep. That's why I brought you here where there's no incentive whatever to remain indoors. All the pleasure and fun and beauty of the place can be had only by remaining *out* in virtually all weathers. This little hotel's as barren of any interest inside as a barrack. No one comes here except to fish and hunt. But Billy Tate is a fine old chap, and he and his wife will take as good care of you as if you were their own. And you remember I told you they have a granddaughter about your age living with them, so you won't lack for company."

Merwin listened in silence.

"Anyway," she said after a little pause, "I am glad enough that you are taking a vacation too, for a while, and can be with me for at least part of the time... till I get used to it. Oh, Dad dear! How I wish you could stay more than four little weeks!"

"I haven't taken three days off for the last four years, so it's going to be *some* vacation for me!" laughed Dr. Scott. "But don't be surprised or disappointed if I'm called back before that for some unexpected operation or other," he added. "A surgeon always has to count on that, you know. However, I'm not anticipating trouble but am looking forward to four wonderful weeks of uninterrupted fishing. Now we ought to get back to the hotel, as Billy Tate has a special lunch ready for us, so he said."

They turned and scrambled down the dune, facing the ruffled blue expanse of Barnegat Bay a short distance to the west. A path of planks led up to the front door of the house and on each side of these planks, great nets were spread to dry on the sand. Over the front steps a dim, weather-beaten sign proclaimed to all concerned that this was "Tate's Hotel," and Dr. Scott told Merwin that this particular stretch of sand and dunes had been known as

"Tate's Beach" since time immemorial, as the father and grandfather of the present proprietor had kept a hostelry here dating back almost to Revolutionary days.

There was little inside the place to remind one that it was a hotel. Indeed, a more informal establishment Merwin had never imagined. The big lobby, or main room, was heated by an immense stove in the center, around which clustered a number of wooden armchairs, all of them now vacant. Several pairs of great rubber hip boots ornamented one corner, and fishing-rods of all descriptions leaned against the walls. A frieze of an odd variety of fishing and hunting trophies also adorned the walls, among which stood out prominently a large and vicious-looking shark's tooth and several great fish glazed and mounted on polished wood.

Over in a corner was a battered desk and behind it a number of wooden pigeon holes, evidently intended to hold mail. And at the desk sat Billy Tate, ruddy, fat, good-natured proprietor of this fisherman's paradise. Merwin had met him a few moments before, when she first entered with her father. But she had escaped to wander off and get a view of the ocean while Billy and her father were exchanging greetings and reminiscences of old times. For Dr. Scott had spent many summer vacations here as a boy.

Billy rose now and waddled toward them.

"Guess the young lady'd like to see my wife and be taken to her room," he remarked, aiming toward another door. "Hey, Susan!" he bawled down a passage. "Here's the folks! Better show 'em their rooms."

After an interval Mrs. Tate appeared. She was as thin and angular as her husband was plump and round. And where he was almost completely bald, her hair was white and abundant. She had, so Merwin thought, the kindliest blue eyes in the world, and the girl liked her immediately. Wiping her hands on a checked apron, Mrs. Tate greeted the newcomers cordially and led them upstairs to their rooms.

It was something of a shock to Merwin to realize that she was to live for several months in this plain, bare little room, as severe as an anchorite's cell. A white iron bedstead, two hard wooden chairs, a battered little bureau with a mirror that screwed one's features into unbelievable contortions, a washstand with white bowl and pitcher, and one rickety little table comprised the whole furnishing. But she soon discovered that the bed was springy and comfortable, the blankets warm and plentiful, the linen clean, and that the two windows looked out on the ocean, over the dunes.

"I put you in here because it's the most comfortable room we have," announced Mrs. Tate, still hovering about her guest. "See, here in the corner is a register leading right up from the stove in the big room downstairs. You'll always be warm enough, I guess, for the fire never goes out there at this season. Now come down and get the lunch I fixed for you."

Dr. Scott and Merwin ate at the one long table in the dining room, capable of seating twenty people, but set for only six or seven.

"Anyone here at present?" the doctor asked of Billy, who had waddled in to keep them company.

"Three or four—off fishin' now. All old-timers. You'll know 'em when you see 'em again: Jenkins and Presby and Dillon and old Doc Trenway. More comin' later, but season's dull this year. Business is bad, and they can't get away for vacations. How'd ye like a little more of these here creamed clams?"

Merwin, whose appetite was never large at the best, could eat scarcely anything now, so busy was she looking about and taking in every detail of her strange new surroundings. They were quite different from anything she had ever known before. From the time she lost her mother when she was ten, her life had been passed mainly at boarding schools, except when she spent the summer months with an aunt, generally at some mountain resort. Of her father, a busy and successful Philadelphia surgeon, she saw little, though she adored him and thought about him and wrote to him continually when she was not with him. But ill health had made it imperative for her to have a distinct change in her mode of life, and her father had decided on the experiment of having her live out of doors on this almost deserted stretch of Jersey coast for a few months. And that she should not begin the experience alone, he had managed to arrange a long-deferred vacation for himself during which he might watch in her the first effects of the change and incidentally indulge in his favorite sport of surf fishing.

Presently, Merwin leaned over to her father and murmured:

"I thought you said the Tates had a granddaughter here about my age. I wonder where she is. I'd like to see her."

Billy caught the remark and chuckled.

"So ye want to see that gran'daughter o' mine!" he said. "Well, you'll see her when she gits tame enough to hover 'round a spell. She's a wild bird, is Peggy!—scared to death of everyone at first, till she gits kinder used to 'em. Never sees any comp'ny much 'cept the fishermen that come here. She ain't seen a girl since I dunno how long. She'll be a good pal, though, once she gits acquainted. There she is now!"

He pointed through one of the windows and Merwin had a glimpse of a little figure flying along over the top of the dunes, her skirts whipped about in the east wind, a mop of beautiful bronze hair streaming out in a thick mane. She seemed to be casting anxious glances toward the house, and Merwin felt sure she would turn and come toward it when she approached the plank walk. But she did not. For one brief moment she seemed to hesitate, then turned away and disappeared in the direction of the ocean.

"Ye see?" said Billy. "She knew ye was comin' an' she's crazy to see ye, but wild horses won't haul her back to the house before nightfall. She's a strange little tike. Always has been."

He went on to talk to Dr. Scott about other matters, and Peggy was apparently forgotten by the two men. But Merwin could not get that flying, wind-blown figure out of her mind and thought about the girl much of the afternoon. Her father went off later with Billy to consider fishing possibilities, and Merwin was left to her own devices. Dr. Scott had suggested that she take a nap, but during an hour spent in wooing sleep, she found it impossible even to close her eyes, so she went out again by herself to ramble on the dunes, hoping to glimpse again the shy, bronze-haired girl who might in time become her companion. Once she thought she saw her peeping out from among some bay bushes, but when she had reached the spot, there was not a soul to be seen.

Late in the afternoon, her father joined her, and they walked up as far as the Coast Guard station, though they did not go in, as it was nearing suppertime.

"You must visit this place tomorrow," said Dr. Scott. "It's interesting to see the workings of one of these stations, and the old captain who runs this one is a good friend of mine. Billy says the men here are all a fine lot, too. There's one of them now."

But Merwin was not interested, just at this time, in the Coast Guard station. She had something else on her mind, and presently she put a question to her father.

"Dad, why do you suppose that granddaughter of Mr. Tate's is so ... sort of ... shy?"

"Well," answered Dr. Scott thoughtfully, "she has a strange history, that little girl, and considering the life she's led, her shyness isn't surprising. To begin with, she isn't really Billy's granddaughter at all—no relation to him, in fact. But she doesn't know this, and you must never tell her. It's a secret that Billy wishes kept from her. Not many know it, but he told me once in a moment of confidence."

"But who *is* she, then?" marveled Merwin.

"A little sea waif, cast up here one night from a terrible wreck. She was saved alive, somehow or other, but everyone else on the vessel was lost, so she was left, so far as we know, without a relative in the world. It happened that Billy Tate's son, who was then one of the Coast Guards here, had recently lost a little girl not much older than this one. The wife, who was living here with the Tates, had been so wild with grief that they feared she would lose her mind. So they gave her this little waif of the sea to take care of, and she soon grew so fond of her that she and her husband decided to adopt her in place of their own. Which they did. A few years later, Billy's son lost his life one night trying to rescue people from a wreck during some wild storm, and the wife lived only a few months after him. So little Peggy was again left an orphan for Billy and his wife to bring up. And here on this lonely beach, she has been brought up ever since."

"But hasn't she ever gone to school or anything like that?" queried Merwin.

"She never had up to the time she was nine or ten," Dr. Scott replied, "and then some of us persuaded Billy that she really ought to have some schooling, somehow or other. But, you see, the difficulty is that there aren't any schools anywhere in this vicinity, for miles on miles. Billy thought it over and decided that we were right and made arrangements to send her to Toms River, have her board there with an old sea captain and his wife who were friends of his, and go to school there. So Peggy went, but the experiment didn't work out well. The child was so lonesome and homesick for the old life that she grew absolutely ill and finally had to be sent back.

"Then, a little later, a man who was principal of a big school in Philadelphia came down to Billy's to stay for several months to recuperate from a severe illness. He took a great interest in little Peggy, discovered that she was really a very bright child, and devoted many weeks to starting her on her education. And I understand that she made very rapid progress, learned to read anything and everything, and tucked away some rudiments of arithmetic besides. But her teacher had to leave, and that's all the schooling Miss Peggy has ever had. A strange life! She's fifteen now and hasn't the faintest notion what it means to live like any ordinary girl of her age. I shall be curious to see how you get on with her. You're the first girl companion she's ever had."

They walked on for a while in silence after this, Merwin's mind full of the strange details of this girl's singular life. So absorbed in her thoughts was she that she scarcely noticed that they were nearing Billy Tate's hotel once more till she suddenly looked up and caught sight of something standing out against the western sky at the point of the tallest dune.

"Look, Daddy! What's that?" she cried, indicating the curious shaft silhouetted against the sunset.

"That? Oh, that's the Northumbrian figurehead!" answered Dr. Scott.

CHAPTER II

At the Foot of the Figurehead

PEGGY TATE HAD had a most exciting day. Curiosity, fear, and eager anticipation had contended with one another, from early morn till dark, for possession of her swiftly beating heart. A strange girl was coming—*a girl!*—to stay right here at the hotel, her own home, and for an indefinite length of time!

Peggy's one experience with girls had been limited to her two weeks' stay at Toms River and her attendance at the public school there. It had not been a pleasant experience. To begin with, she had been breaking her heart for her own home and her loving grandfather and grandmother. Old Captain Sawyer and his wife had been very kind, but she had felt like a little wild animal caught in a trap whose captors were trying to be gentle and soothe her anguish. And she was just about as responsive as such a wild creature would have been.

Then the school . . . and the memory of those awful,

strange boys and girls!... They had glanced at her sideways and giggled and made half-audible remarks behind their hands—remarks in which "Redhead!" stood out with glaring distinctness. One or two girls had made a feeble effort to be friendly and offered to lend her pencils and erasers, had even come over to eat their lunch with her. But she soon discovered that their apparent kindness only covered an insatiable curiosity to hear all about who she was and where she came from. And when she did not respond to their prying questions with sufficient promptness, they speedily deserted her.

The teacher might in time have gained her confidence, but the poor woman was overworked and harassed by a too-large class and could give virtually no individual attention to anyone. So the little bronze-haired, wistful-eyed child was overlooked till it was too late to think about her, for in two weeks' time the bewildered old captain was advised by the doctor to send her back to her home.

Thus had Peggy Tate been forced to have no opinion at all of girls. Yet, curiously enough, she still longed with an unspeakable longing for a girl companion who would be all to her that she desired. And now one was coming! What would *she* be like? Grandfather Tate could furnish no information, for he had never seen Merwin Scott, scarcely knew of her existence, in fact. The families of his fishing friends were in the main an unknown quantity to him, unless they happened to have sons to be initiated into the sacred rites performed on the fishing beach. He could only tell Peggy that he liked the girl's father.

"Doc Scott's a fine man," he declared. "None better. He's a number one! So if his darter ain't fine, she must be pretty unnatural; that's all I know about it."

And with this Peggy had had to be content.

The morning had passed in feverish watching for the motorboat that was to bring the stranger across the bay from Toms River, this particular beach being inaccessible by any other means of locomotion. While, from behind a convenient screen of bushes, she watched the landing place, Peggy debated what would be her line of conduct in case she did not like the appearance of this new arrival. Should she ignore her existence and continue to live as though the stranger had never materialized? This would scarcely be possible considering the close proximity in which they would have to live. And besides, her grandparents probably would not like it, particularly if they were fond of the girl's father.

No, she would have to recognize this new girl's existence to a certain extent, but the acquaintanceship need not be an intimate one or go any further than she, Peggy, cared to have it go. But if she *did* like her—well, that was another matter! At any rate, she had made up her mind to go very cautiously about becoming friendly. She would make no advances. Let the other girl do that!

Then the launch arrived. From behind her bushes, Peggy watched anxiously while the newcomers disembarked on the little wharf. The doctor she already knew—and liked, though she had not seen him in several years. He had once attended her during a short but rather critical illness she had had while he was down on one of his fishing trips. She had never forgotten how faithfully he had watched over her till the crisis was past, foregoing the pleasure of his short vacation, nor the pleased expression in his kind brown eyes when he knew that she was at least out of danger.

So this was his daughter—this slender, light-haired, pale young person at his side! Peggy parted the bushes to get a better view. She was near enough to hear Merwin's voice and was held by its low, throaty, musical quality. But when Merwin held on to her father's arm a little unsteadily in walking along the narrow, two-planked dock to which she was quite unused (being also a trifle dizzy at times since her recent illness), Peggy Tate straightway put her down as being affected and citified.

"She's stuck up!" thought Peggy. "Pretends to be scared about a little thing like that. I'm going to hate her, I guess!" The impression was intensified when, a few minutes later, Merwin came out by herself to look about from the top of the dunes and was joined by Dr. Scott. Peggy, behind another clump of bushes now, heard the doctor ask his daughter if she liked it, heard Merwin's reply that she didn't know, it was so wild and lonely. That was enough! Of course she didn't and wouldn't like it, raged Peggy to herself. How could a city girl like this life, anyway, and why had she come here? She scrambled noiselessly away without waiting to hear any more.

Later in the afternoon, when she happened to go into the kitchen, Mrs. Tate said to her:

"Why've you been runnin' around all mornin' like a wild thing, Peggy? That new girl's come and you ought to get acquainted with her. She's lonesome. Nice little thing, too. She's lyin' down now, like Doc told her to, but you take her out this afternoon and make her feel at home. You'n she ought to be good friends."

Lying down, was she? Another city affectation, thought Peggy, though not precisely in those terms. She sniffed scornfully as she ate a cold biscuit and some peach-plum jam. But she waited about dutifully till she heard Merwin coming downstairs again, when shyness seized her once more and she slipped away by a back door and was out of sight before Mrs. Tate realized she was going. Nevertheless, she watched Merwin during her stroll, keeping skillfully out of sight behind the dunes till the doctor had joined his daughter and escorted her up toward the Coast Guard station. Then Peggy went about her own affairs.

Had the tables been turned and had anyone been watching Peggy, he would then have been considerably bewildered at the performance about to be witnessed. Peggy scrambled along behind the dunes till she came to the highest one and clambered up the slippery, shifting sand nearly to its summit. Just below the top, on the bay side, was a rough shack not more than six or seven feet in dimensions and very dilapidated. It had once been used by fishermen for storing nets in, but had evidently long since been abandoned. The little door hung sagging on one hinge and sand had sifted in deeply over the floor.

Into this shack Peggy dived, emerging shortly with a rusty old trowel in her hand.

Up toward the summit of the dune was a curious structure. It was built of heavy ship's timbers, at the rear four or five feet high and as many wide and long. But on the seaward side, the sand of the dune had blown or drifted up clear to the top, so that from the front view there was only a solid platform level with the sand. From this platform rose the wooden bulk of a great figure facing the sea—a woman's figure, some seven feet high, carved to represent draperies blown backward by the wind, hair flying backward too, hands crossed over the breast, and a wild, exultant expression in its really beautiful face. The figure appeared to be leaning far forward and was braced in the back by a great piece of timber like the bowsprit of a ship.

But Peggy was paying no attention to the wooden figure. She had crept to the base of the platform on which it rested and, with the rusty trowel, was digging away furiously at the sand in the rear. Every once in a while she stopped to peer cautiously over the edge of the dune, up and down the beach. Then she would go back to the digging. At last she appeared to have excavated a tunnel under the supports of the platform sufficiently wide enough to insert her arm and hand.

It was a strange assortment of things that she drew out from this tunnel. An onlooker might well have been surprised at the collection, had anyone been near enough to see what they were. But Peggy took care that no one was near. Again and again, she peered over the edge of the dune and scanned the wide reach of the bay behind her. Then she carefully laid out in a row before her some half dozen articles, each of which she took up in turn, spent a long while examining and pondering over, and laid down in its place before she took up another.

When every one had been given a close scrutiny, she sat for some time, chin cupped in hands and elbows on knees, staring thoughtfully at the entire collection, her brows knit in puzzled thought. Suddenly, at the sound of voices, she scrambled them all quickly together and hastily inserted them through the tunnel, filling up the space in the sand with her bare hands when the last one had disappeared. The trowel she threw behind her into the shack and crawled up to look over the dune and see who the intruders might be.

They were, as she had suspected, Dr. Scott and his daughter, trudging through the sand and now quite close to this dune and undoubtedly coming closer. So close, indeed, were they that she had no time to disappear through the bushes without being observed, no time even to slip into the shack and get out of sight. She sat quite still where she was, down beside the pedestal of the figure on the bay side of the dune, feeling trapped at last, but hoping madly to escape notice by keeping very quiet. If they did not come over that side, she might not be seen. There was at least a chance.

She heard Merwin ask her father, "What's that?" and heard him respond that it was "the Northumbrian figurehead." And she hoped that Merwin might not be moved to ask any more questions about it. But Merwin was.

"How curious! I want to see it closer. Do tell me about it, Daddy!" the musical voice continued. And footsteps, crunching through the sand, warned Peggy that discovery was now very near. The two approached the figure from the ocean side, clambering up the dune, and stood before it not ten feet away from where Peggy crouched.

"Where did it come from and how did it get here?" demanded Merwin.

"It was once the figurehead of an old vessel," Dr. Scott explained. "I believe the name of that vessel was *The Northumbria*. It was wrecked off this shore many years ago; I don't know how many, but not in my lifetime, or Billy Tate's either. It may have been as far back as his grandfather's. No one seems to know much about the vessel, but the figurehead was washed ashore and someone—perhaps Billy's grandfather—set it up here on this solid pedestal, just for a whim, evidently. People around here like it and have always been very careful never to allow it to be removed or tampered with. Billy is very proud of it and says there's nothing like it all up and down the coast. He wouldn't part with it for anything you could offer, and we're all rather fond of it." People around here like it and have always been very careful never to allow it to be removed or tampered with.

Merwin had come up very close to the figure and was gazing straight into the beautiful face, whose wooden, sightless eyes seemed to be sweeping the far horizon.

"How strange! But I like it," she said. "I think I'm going to be fond of it, too."

"Come over on this side," went on the doctor, "and you can see how solid the pedestal is on which it rests. The timber it was made of was so durable that no storms or high seas have ever—good gracious! Why, Peggy, child, how you startled me! I never dreamed you were here."

Dr. Scott had almost stumbled over the little crouching figure that was huddled down beside the pedestal, when he stepped over to that side of the dune. The expression of a trapped animal was in Peggy's eyes, but she involuntarily put her hand into the doctor's as he held it out, and his warm, friendly grip somewhat reassured her.

"Well . . . now you must meet my daughter. It's time you two got to know each other," declared the doctor heartily. "Merwin, this is little Miss Peggy, and I hope you two are going to be good friends. I want you to take good care of Merwin, Peggy, for she hasn't been at all well and I've been considerably worried about her. If you help her to get back her health, you'll be doing a big thing for me. Will you?"

He asked it directly and with purpose, gazing straight into Peggy's big gray eyes. He knew only too well that they had taken the girl at a disadvantage, that she was as frightened of them as a little wild hare; also, he felt that it would go a long way toward establishing a friendship between her and Merwin if he could ask for cooperation from Peggy as a direct favor to himself. And his stratagem was successful.

"Yes . . . Dr. Scott," stammered Peggy, and she put her

hand into the one Merwin held out to her, looking up suddenly into Merwin's friendly eyes. Perhaps, after all, she thought, she might get to like this girl. And she had promised the doctor she would take care of her; and a promise was a promise, inviolable and sacred. Whether she liked her or not, that must be kept.

Dr. Scott suddenly remembered a pressing engagement with Billy to get some bait before it was dark. So, making his excuses, he hurried away, leaving the two girls alone, looking uneasily at each other, the great figurehead brooding over them from above. It was Merwin who broke the trying silence at length by remarking:

"She's wonderful, isn't she, standing up alone, here, through all kinds of weather ... sort of ... keeping watch over things. I've never seen anything like her before. I wonder what became of the vessel she used to belong to."

"I ... don't know," responded Peggy, shyly. "Went all to pieces, I s'pose, like they mostly do." In her own mind she was deeply grateful that this new girl had the sense to keep to impersonal subjects like the figurehead and did not begin tormenting her at once by a foolish catechism of endless questions about herself, as the girls in Toms River had done. She was rather attracted, too, by Merwin's pleasant, friendly manner, her well-bred, sensitive face and quiet, deep-blue eyes. Decidedly this was better than she had hoped or feared. She wanted to ask Merwin if she liked the beach, if she knew anything about sailing, fishing, or crabbing, if she had ever seen the lifeboats taken out to some wreck in a heavy storm. She even wanted to ask her if she liked to read, and what books she preferred, and whether or not she had brought any with her. A dozen questions rushed to her own lips, but she was too shy to utter any of them. And while she was struggling to articulate something, Merwin innocently moved round to the back of the figurehead and made a remark that drove Peggy clear back into the fastnesses of her intense reserve again.

"What a strange pedestal this rests on!" observed Merwin. "It's as solid and substantial as a small house. Is it hollow inside, do you think? I wonder if it would be possible to get into it in any way." Her question was asked out of mere idle curiosity, but the effect on Peggy was astonishing. The girl's face flushed a sudden scarlet. She clenched her small fist and stamped a foot in what appeared to be an actual rage.

"Why do you ask? Why do you ask?" she muttered. "Of course you can't get into it! Why should you want to?"

Then, recovering herself and deeply ashamed of her outburst, she turned and ran from Merwin, down the slope to the dune and away toward the hotel, leaving a stunned and wondering new friend behind her, staring after her from the top of the dune.

CHAPTER III

The Mystery of Peggy

ONE MORNING, SOME three days later, Merwin awoke and lay gazing for a while at the rim of the sun creeping up over the horizon above the tossing blue expanse of the sea. It was an enchanting sight, one utterly new to her, and she felt she could never weary of its daily repetition. And while she lay luxuriating in being able to witness all this beauty as she snuggled down into the cozy warmth of her bed, she mentally reviewed the developments of her stay so far at Tate's Hotel.

She was going to like it. Of that she was now absolutely certain. Already she reveled in the rough comfort of the place, the plain but tasteful food (for she had suddenly acquired a marvelous appetite), and the exhilaration of this out-of-door life. But there were other things besides this to enthrall her. She delighted in the long tramps on the beach with her father, the excursions out on the bay in the little motorboat with him and Billy Tate when he chose to try fishing in that direction, the pleasant evenings when the fishermen all gathered about the big stove in the lobby, basked in its welcome heat, and swapped fishing stories or listened to Billy's extraordinary tales of storms and wrecks on this lonely beach.

But most of all she was fascinated by the mystery of Peggy Tate. For mystery there was; of that she could no longer be in doubt. The girl was an absolute enigma to her. The only direct contact she had had with her had been the meeting late that first afternoon and once again yesterday, when quite by chance she had gone into the kitchen for some hot water and found Peggy helping Mrs. Tate fold some clean clothes. She had greeted Peggy warmly and asked her whether she would care to take a walk on the beach later. But the girl had only made some evasive reply and slipped quietly away a few minutes later while Merwin was still talking to Mrs. Tate. The latter had been plainly embarrassed by the singular behavior of her granddaughter and tried anxiously to excuse it.

"She's a strange child, Peggy is!" sighed Mrs. Tate. "I jest can't make her out, sometimes. Seems like she ought to be jest tickled to pieces to have a nice girl like you for a friend. But somehow she ain't used to goin' with no one; jest runs round by herself all the time. But don't you mind, Merwin; she'll come round, all right, by and by, when she gets to know you better."

But this was not all that Merwin had seen of Peggy during the interval. Quite unknown to the girl, she had caught a curious glimpse of Peggy when the latter had thought herself unobserved, and that glimpse had been a mysterious one. On the morning after the Scotts' arrival, Merwin had gone out to explore the region alone—not on the ocean side of the dunes, this time, but over toward the bay, by a path that led through thick undergrowth of bayberry and cedar bushes often much higher than her head. On emerging from one of these and finding herself close to the vicinity of the old figurehead, she beheld a curious sight. On her knees in the sand at the foot of the figurehead's support knelt Peggy, industriously digging away in the sand with what appeared to be a trowel. So furiously and purposefully was she toiling at this task that Merwin unconsciously stopped where she was to watch the proceeding.

When the bronze-haired girl had reached a certain point in the excavation, she put a hand and arm into a hole at the foot of the pedestal and drew out, one after another, a singular array of articles. From that distance, Merwin could not see distinctly what they all were. Two that most excited her curiosity were what looked like a tiny child's garment (Peggy had shaken it out and refolded it) and a little red-bound book of some kind that she tucked into the folds of the dress. The other things were small and not distinguishable from where Merwin stood. All these articles Peggy held in her lap. After she had filled in the hole again, she gathered up her skirt and rose, looking about her uneasily as if seeking another hiding place for her treasures. She even walked off a few feet with them, in a direction away from the hotel.

Then she did a peculiar thing—to Merwin an amazing thing. For, instead of going on, she suddenly turned back, flung herself down by the figurehead again, began to dig rapidly in the same spot, and presently reinterred the articles in precisely the same place from which she had taken them. When they were all hidden from sight and the hole filled up with sand, she knelt before the timbers of the figurehead's support and seemed to be frantically striving to erase something from one of the boards. She even dug at it with the trowel and rubbed it with sand. Later, after a dissatisfied survey of her work, she ran off down the beach and disappeared behind the dunes.

It had all been quite incomprehensible to Merwin. She had a guilty feeling that she ought not to be watching the girl, and yet for the life of her she could not withdraw her fascinated gaze. Her first impulse, after Peggy had run off, was to dash over to the figurehead and try to find out what it was all about. But this she felt would be a sort of treachery to the girl whose friendship she really wanted to gain. So, stifling her intense curiosity, she went for a long stroll in another direction.

It had not been till yesterday afternoon that she passed the figurehead again in the course of a ramble along the beach. This time she felt quite justified in going close to it, even walking around it and surveying it with intent gaze from the back. The sun, setting over the bay, threw level rays across to the timbers of the massive support, and, without any effort, Merwin could discern very clearly the exact spot at which Peggy had worked so energetically the day before. The timber was splintered where she had hacked at it with the trowel. But under the splintering Merwin plainly perceived what she had not noticed before—the remains of a little Maltese cross, not more than two inches in extent, still visible in dim black paint, old and weatherworn and all but erased by time.

"Now, what in the world," thought Merwin as she lay in her warm bed and watched the sun creep farther and farther up over the sea, "could she have been trying to do to that little mark? It must be that she wanted to make it disappear somehow, but what for? Can it be possible she was trying to conceal it from *me*?" And at the shock of this possibility, Merwin sat straight up in bed and with a bewildered gesture pushed her thick light hair back from her forehead.

"I do believe Peggy *hates* me!" she thought suddenly. "But why? I never did her any harm, and I'm just crazy to be friends with her. Why can't she understand it? I wonder—" she buried her face in her hands a moment and thought hard, "I wonder if she can possibly think I'm trying to find out her secret . . . whatever it is. I did make an awfully unfortunate remark, that first afternoon when Daddy and I found her there. We were getting along nicely till I said something about that place under the figurehead being hollow, perhaps, and asked if one could get in there . . . I remember now. She went right off the handle and hasn't said a word to me since. Yes, I do believe that's it. She thinks I want to find out her secret. How perfectly silly! As if I could possibly have known she had one!"

THE MYSTERY OF PEGGY

At this point, Merwin drew out her little watch from under the pillow and found it was high time to get up. But while she was dressing, she continued to review the subject of Peggy's strange conduct and made two resolutions: first that she would win Peggy's confidence if it were humanly possible, and second, that she would not tell her father of the girl's strange conduct till she had, herself, made further progress unraveling the mystery. The determination added zest and interest to the quiet, wholesome life she had begun to lead. Had she but known it, the day was destined to be crowded with unexpected adventure and mystery.

It began by her coming face to face with Peggy, alone on the dunes, that morning shortly after breakfast. Dr. Scott had gone off for a day's fishing alone with Billy and had left Merwin to her own devices. As the morning was sunny, even hot for October, she had elected to spend it sitting on the dunes with a book. To this end she had gone out with a steamer rug and her book and established herself on the height of the dune at the foot of the figurehead. This location she had chosen, not with any intention, but simply because of the fascination the great draped figure had for her.

But she found that she could not read. The sea lay like a floor of blue at her feet. A low, lazy surf broke almost like a ripple on the yellow sand. The white-and-red shaft of Barnegat Light stood out sharply against a deep-blue sky. Seagulls swooped and dived. And over her head the great figure brooded. Who could read with so much beauty to distract the attention? Merwin sat with chin cupped in her hands, gazing seaward like the figure above her and thinking of nothing in particular, not even of Peggy, when she was startled by a rustling sound back of her. She quickly turned to find Peggy gazing at her from around the base of the figurehead with a decidedly hostile expression in her big gray eyes.

"Hello!" said Merwin amiably. "That you, Peggy? Do come and sit down and talk to me a while. I'm awfully lonely." She said it rather wistfully, for she was truly anxious to gain the friendship of this strange girl and was indeed lonely and bored with her own companionship. Perhaps Peggy perceived the wistfulness, for her expression grew less hostile. But she demanded quite surprisingly:

"Why did you come and sit right here?"

Somewhat taken aback, Merwin replied:

"I honestly don't know, Peggy. I didn't choose this spot for any particular reason, except that I sort of like this old figurehead. She's company ... somehow." Peggy appeared rather startled by this remark, but made no comment. And Merwin suddenly determined to take a bold stand and find out if possible what was in the mind of this strange child.

"Why don't you want to be friends with me, Peggy?" she demanded. "Have I done anything to offend you? If so, I truly didn't mean it. It certainly was unintentional."

The effect of this declaration on the bronze-haired girl was rather curious. Surprise, incredulity, suspicion, all ranged over her expressive little face. Then, with a softer look in her eyes, she ventured:

"I thought you didn't want to be friends and . . . and . . . well, never mind what else I thought. It had something to do with this figurehead . . . but I guess maybe it's all right. . . . What's the book you got there?" And her angry gaze focused on the volume in Merwin's lap.

"It's a mystery story, *The Circular Staircase*. Have you ever read it? I love mystery stories, and Daddy lets me read some of the good ones. Do you like them?"

"I never read any," was Peggy's rather surprising statement. "But I'd like to!" she added and then, a little breathlessly: "You don't always have to *read* about mysteries. Sometimes they're right here—right in your life."

Merwin stared at her in astonishment. Then she managed to stammer:

"Oh! . . . do you think so, Peggy? Have you . . ."

But Peggy had already repented of her candor, for she flushed a sudden scarlet, turned away abruptly, and without another word ran off down the dune in the direction of the bay.

"Oh, me!" thought Merwin, gazing after her regretfully. "What can be the matter now? I hope I haven't offended her again. But what can she mean about the mystery business? Anyhow, I've made some progress in talking to her. Maybe she'll thaw out sometime. I've almost finished with this book, and I'll give it to her this afternoon. Perhaps that'll help her to feel more friendly."

All the rest of the morning she watched by the figurehead, hoping that Peggy would reappear and resume her friendly attitude. But Peggy remained invisible, and Merwin finally finished her book and strolled back to dinner, which she ate alone in the big dining room, as all the others were off for the day fishing.

After dinner she went to take her daily nap, and on the way to her room she stepped in and laid the book on the bed in the room next to hers, which she had discovered was Peggy's. Between its leaves she had placed a little note which ran:

Keep this as long as you like, Peggy. I've finished it. And I have some more books for you when you want them.
Merwin

Later in the afternoon, as it was still warm and attractive outdoors, she decided to take a long stroll along the beach toward the lighthouse, a direction in which she had not yet explored. At first she walked along the edge of the sea, hardly having to change her course a foot to escape the surf that was rolling in so lazily. But after a while, deciding that this was tame sport, she climbed to the top of the dunes instead and proceeded on her way, scrambling through the wiry high grass and scrub growth that fringed the tops, clambering up and down the heights as the dunes rose and fell, getting scratched and disheveled but enjoying the rough journey more than she would have imagined such a thing possible a month before.

Over toward the west, the bay was lit with a glory of waning afternoon sun. And presently, at a certain spot down near the edge of the water on that side, she spied a great clump of late pink marshmallow, flaunting blossoms too beautiful to be ignored.

"I'll go get those," she told herself. "Daddy loves them, and these are probably the last there'll be *this* year. He'll be delighted to see them on the table tonight."

Down the dune she scrambled, through the thick bay bushes, across a marshy bog in which, though she skipped over the grassy tufts, she managed to get her feet pretty wet, and so over to the edge of the bay. On nearing the spot, she found that the marshmallows grew on the other side of a sandy pool and would be quite unattainable unless she took off her ties and stockings and waded across the shallow water. Having come thus far, however, Merwin refused to be daunted by so simple an affair, so she slipped them off and stepped cautiously into the pool.

"Somehow this sand feels very soft and shifting," she thought as she proceeded toward the center. "I wonder what's the matter with it."

At the next step, her foot sank down above the ankle and as she tried to pull it back, the other went down over the knee. For neither foot now was there the slightest foundation of solidity. Floundering about in a frantic effort to extricate herself, or at least get nearer to the edge of the bank, she realized with utter horror that she was caught—caught without help or hope in a strange, bottomless bog into which she was sinking more deeply each moment.

"Oh, Daddy, Daddy!" she moaned. "Can't you come to me? Where are you? I . . . I can't get out of here!"

Another floundering struggle resulted only in her plunging to her waist in the deceitful shifting sand.

"Help! Help!" she screamed, the agonized terror of the very worst lending a piercing shrillness to her voice.

The cry of a swooping seagull over her head was the only answer to her call.

CHAPTER IV

Peggy Changes Her Mind

PEGGY SAT ON the little dock that stretched out into the bay, her feet dangling over the water. In her lap lay an open book, and on its pages her eyes were focused as she read with deep and breathless interest. Peggy was lost to the world in the mystery of *The Circular Staircase*.

She had found the book on her bed that afternoon with Merwin's note tucked between the leaves. At first she had been inclined to be suspicious of it and had turned the pages over with a rather scornful stare. But interesting words and sentences soon gripped her, and before she realized it, she was deeply absorbed and had read nearly half a chapter. Then she succumbed, took the book out with her, and sat on the dock to enjoy the thrilling tale.

Once only she glanced up, to perceive Merwin starting out apparently on a walk by herself, disappearing across the dunes in the direction of the lighthouse. Just for an instant, Peggy was half inclined to call to her and offer to accompany her, possibly out of sheer gratitude for Merwin's kindness in lending the book. But the unfolding story was too fascinating. She must get on with it. Another time would do to walk with Merwin. She dropped her eyes again to the book.

Time flew by and the afternoon waned. The sun drew down toward the west, and its level rays shone straight into Peggy's eyes so that she shifted her position to the side of the dock in order to avoid it. The story gripped her interest more and more. Yet, in spite of it, an uneasy feeling began to take hold of her that all was not well somehow. It was a feeling that she was rather at a loss to explain. She even put the book aside for a moment to argue the question out with herself. There was nothing she was supposed to be doing just at that time. She had shelled the beans for supper and peeled the potatoes. It was not yet time to go up and set the table. Nor could she remember any commands or requests from Grandma Tate. No, there was nothing to prevent her sitting there comfortably and reading that enthralling book. What was it, then, that bothered her?

And she considered further that at least, engaged in this occupation, she did not fear the sudden appearance of that girl, Merwin. And now her thoughts were turned in that direction, she began to wonder just where the girl had gone on her ramble and whether or not she was back yet. It was getting late, and she had heard Dr. Scott warn his daughter not to be out roaming about too late on the beach, as there were dangers that might threaten her, unaccustomed as she was to the locality. Perhaps he would rather expect Peggy to accompany her when she went off on a long stroll as she evidently had today.

And then Peggy suddenly remembered her promise to Dr. Scott and the expression in his brown eyes when he had asked her to take good care of Merwin. And the guilty feeling grew in her that she hadn't kept that promise very well—not at all, in fact, so far. To be sure, Merwin had not needed any care, until now, as she had seemed to stay pretty closely in the region of the hotel. But even so, Peggy realized that she had not been kind, had deliberately avoided the company of the new girl, and had ignored every effort of hers to be friendly. Dr. Scott would not approve of that and would think her ungrateful if nothing worse.

After these reflections the book ceased to hold her. She found she could no longer concentrate her mind on it, so she closed it, got to her feet, and went up to the hotel to see if Merwin had returned. She had not, and Mrs. Tate was beginning to fuss about her and was inclined to be irritable with Peggy.

"You don't treat that girl right, Peggy child!" she complained. "Doc Scott wouldn't like it a bit if he knew, and I'm more'n half inclined to tell him. 'Tain't kind to leave her runnin' around like that by herself an' you could jest as well go with her as not. She might get lost any time in that there scrub undergrowth or fall inter something or goodness knows what. You go this minute and hunt her up. Do you know which way she went?"

Peggy nodded and pointed down toward the lighthouse.

"I'll go find her, all right!" she announced and was off before Mrs. Tate could say anything more.

Along the top of the dunes ran Peggy, winged now by a guilty conscience and by some obscure fear that reason for which she could not fathom. As she could get the best view on both sides from the top of the dunes, she kept to them, scanning both the ocean beach and the edge of the bay. On neither was there a sign of the girl she sought. The sun had by now almost touched the horizon and cast deep shadows where the high bushes and scrub-cedar growth intercepted its light.

"Merwin! Merwin!" Peggy began to shout at length, for she feared that the girl might escape her in the waning light. There was no answer to her shouts; nevertheless she continued to call at intervals till her voice was hoarse from the effort.

A mile . . . two miles, she hurried along, unknowingly following precisely the same track that Merwin had taken earlier in the afternoon. And a sort of discouragement began to settle down on her. Even as she panted on, she reasoned with herself that this was all probably very silly, that Merwin had no doubt long since returned, and that she had missed her in some thick growth of the bushes farther along the beach. Merwin was no doubt even now comfortably back at the hotel, while she, Peggy, was scrambling wildly over the dunes in a fool's chase of her. She would go no farther but return, herself, and see whether the girl had got back. If not she could start out afresh.

As she thought this, she halted on a high dune, swept both sides with a keen glance, and once more lifted her hoarse voice to call Merwin's name. And at the same moment, a thrill shot through her, for she thought she detected an answering cry—a faint, a very faint, call that sounded like "*Help!*" Again she scanned the ocean beach and turned to the bay side, raising her voice once more in an anxious cry: "Merwin! Are you there?" This time not a sound or an echo responded. But her eye was caught by the flaunting group of pink marshmallows, picked out by the last rays of the vanishing sun, and instantly a horrible thought came to Peggy.

They flanked the edge of a quicksand pool, of which there were a few in the vicinity along the bay side. Some of them were harmless, mere shallow stretches of shifting, unstable sand. Two or three were extremely dangerous, capable of sucking one down to unplumbed depths; this she knew was one of the dangerous ones. Grandfather Tate had several times warned her against it, and she had once tested it herself with an old harpoon stuck straight down, as far out as she could reach. The iron had completely disappeared, and she had never discovered to what depth it had sunk. If Merwin had strayed into that terrible pool . . . !

Panic-stricken now, she clambered down the dune, caught her foot in the wild vine, fell, scrambled up again, and hurried on through the marshy bog, caring not whether she trod on the hummocks or in the mud, calling every other moment: "Merwin! *Merwin!*" Her voice seemed to have the quality she had noticed once or twice in a nightmare dream when she had tried and tried to scream and could not, no matter what the effort. As she fought her way through a thick tangle of bushes and emerged in the open on the other side, she noticed an old broken oar lying half-buried in the sand. Almost without conscious volition she stooped and picked it up, carrying it with her although it hampered her progress not a little.

When she arrived at the edge of the pool, she was breathless with exertion and shaking like a leaf. Had Merwin quite disappeared? Was there no hope? But yes, there she was, sunk to the armpits, thrashing feebly at the shallow water with both hands but making no outcry now. Peggy's heart gave a terrible leap and almost stood still. Was she ... *could* she be beyond the reach of that broken oar? Would she be too weak, too exhausted to grasp it?

"Merwin!" she cried, standing on the solid ground not fifteen feet away from the sinking girl, "Don't struggle so much. It only makes you sink deeper. I'm going to push an oar out to you. See if you can catch hold of it ... and then hold on *tight*."

The desperate eyes of the sinking girl turned to her rescuer as if she saw her for the first time.

"Oh, Peggy! I thought I heard you ... or someone ... call. But I wasn't sure. I couldn't answer loud. My voice is all gone." It was indeed nothing more than a faint croak by this time. "Can I ever get out of here?"

"Don't talk," commanded Peggy, "but just do as I tell you. I'm going to try to reach this oar out to you. Hold on to it tight when you get it. I'll see whether I can pull you out."

Lying flat on the solid ground, Peggy edged the oar out farther and farther in the shallow water, and Merwin, who, fortunately, was turned halfway facing her, stretched her arm to its utmost. But she was still more than a foot away from the end of the broken oar blade. Not with the utmost exertion at either end could it possibly be made to span the distance. With a little groan Peggy called:

"Wait a moment. I'll see if I can find something better."

She dashed away into the bushes and Merwin was again left alone, sinking inch by inch as she distinctly realized. Though, heeding Peggy's warning about not struggling, she did not sink quite as rapidly as before. Would her rescuer never come back? Was she doomed, after all, to go down into this horrible place with human aid so near and yet so useless? But there was Peggy calling. She could not see her now, in the waning twilight, but she could hear the words:

"Cheer up, Merwin. I got something else!"

Presently she saw Peggy emerging from the bushes, slowly, dragging something behind her that appeared to require all her strength. After what seemed an interminable age, the girl got to the edge of the quicksand, hauling a long, thick, round piece of timber that looked as if it might have been the boom or spar of some sailing vessel. It must have been twelve or fifteen feet long and was plainly more than she could have managed in ordinary circumstances.

"I ... found ... this ... Merwin!" she panted, almost too exhausted to drag it any farther. "Just a minute ...

till I get . . . my breath . . . and I'll shove it . . . out to you." At the same time, her quick eyes had noted that Merwin was perceptibly deeper than when she had left her. There was not a moment to lose. With incredible strength for one so slight, she pushed the long spar out, inch by inch, foot by foot, till miraculously the end was within reach of Merwin's hand. Feebly the sinking girl grasped it and hung on with a great sigh of relief. Peggy kept her end well on the solid ground and finally sat on it so that it might remain the more steady and not sink at the end out in the pool.

"Oh, Peggy!" gasped Merwin after a time. "This didn't come a moment too soon. I was sinking over my shoulders. I think in another minute my arms would have gone under. I can raise myself a little on this. But I'm afraid I can't pull myself out. I'm in too deep. What shall I do now?"

"Wait a minute, if you're all right, and let me think," said Peggy. "I can't pull this back with your weight on it, but if you can hang on, I'll try to do something else." She sat for several minutes on her end of the spar, her set, determined little face turned toward the last afterglow of twilight in the west, trying desperately to think out the next move. It would never do to leave Merwin alone long enough to go back to the hotel for help. Nor was there much hope that even if they were missed, as they doubtless must be by now, any help could reach them inside of an hour or so. Her grandfather and Dr. Scott were in all probability not yet home from their fishing trip. The other men might or might not have come in. There was no one that Mrs. Tate could send to aid them, short of the Coast Guard station that was fully three-quarters of a mile away in the opposite direction from the hotel. The situation was certainly rather desperate.

Suddenly, at the thought of the Coast Guard station, another idea popped into her mind. She turned to Merwin with a note of renewed hope in her voice.

"See if you can hold on to that end without me sitting on this one," she commanded. "If it doesn't sink down too much and will hold you, I have another idea." She rose and watched the effect of leaving the spar unbalanced at her own end, and found that though it sank a trifle at the other end, it seemed to be heavy enough to bear Merwin's weight without going under, probably because there were several feet of it on shore.

"Yes, it'll do," decided Peggy. "Now you can wait here while I go across the dune to the ocean side. The Coast Guard that patrols the beach will be walking along this way in just a few minutes. It's time for him right now, I should say. I'll watch for him and get him to come over and the two of us can probably dig you out. You don't mind waiting alone, do you?"

"Yes, I mind awfully," acknowledged Merwin, in a weak voice. "But it's got to be done, so you go ahead, Peggy. Only ... only I hope it won't be ... too long. I'll try to hold on, but I'm beginning to feel so strange ... and sort of faint."

With deep misgivings at this new development, Peggy started off, and the falling darkness almost immediately shut her from Merwin's sight.

CHAPTER XIV

The First Results

I WISH YOU YOUNGSTERS had seen fit to let me in a little earlier on this affair," remarked Dr. Scott to Merwin next morning in a few spare moments they had to themselves. "My vacation is considerably more than half over, and I rather hate to go back leaving the riddle unsolved."

"Can you make anything of it?" Merwin asked curiously.

"Not much just yet, but I have several conjectures that may lead to something. There's more in this thing than meets the eye at first glance. In fact, I think you girls have stumbled on a pretty neat little mystery. If Peggy only were not so set on not having anyone else let into the secret, I might be able to make much quicker progress, but the child seems determined that it must go no further than the three of us. I may be able to make her change her mind later, but just now I don't want to push her a bit further than she is willing to go.

"One thing I have done, however, for I felt that the time had unquestionably come when it must be done. Last night I had a long talk with Billy and warned him that Peggy suspects a good many things about her not being his own grandchild. I did this in such a way as not to violate her confidence in regard to what she found under the figurehead. I put it on the ground of what old Captain Wareham had told me, and I also said that you thought she was worrying over the matter. I told him that it would be much better for her, and set his mind at ease too, if he would just quietly find the opportunity to tell her the truth about herself, so far as he knew it.

"If," Dr. Scott went on, "Peggy realized that she had been legally adopted and was in the sight of the law no different from an own child and was quite as truly beloved, she would soon get used to the idea and after a while forget all her terrors of the subject. I told him, besides, that neither she nor he would ever have a moment's peace while the matter hung in the wind this way; that she evidently suspected too much, and that it might seriously affect her health if she worried any more about it. He agreed with me, finally, and decided to have it out with her this morning. So don't be surprised at any change you may see in her later. That was my first step in the matter. It will probably clear the way for later developments."

It did. And in a rather surprising manner. Peggy came to Merwin's room when she was lying down that afternoon and shut the door in a very mysterious way.

"I want to tell you something," she said. "I've found out all about it!"

"Found out about what?" inquired Merwin, trying to make her intonation sound sufficiently surprised, though indeed she felt no surprise at what she knew Peggy was about to disclose. Her only wonder was as to how the girl would take her discovery.

"Grandpa Tate had a long talk with me this morning. He told me that he thought the time had come when I should know all about myself. He said he was afraid I might discover it in some other way and be frightened about it. It's so—just as I thought. I *was* that baby, the one that was brought ashore that night from the wreck. They never could find out who I was or anything about me, so they just adopted me in place of the baby they'd lost. They did it by law, somehow, so that I'm just the same as their own and nobody could ever take me away from them. . . . Oh, Merwin, I'm so glad!—glad that I know for sure now! I was always so afraid that . . . perhaps . . . sometime a stranger would come along and . . . and claim me and . . . take me away from them. It's all right now. I don't care so much any more. But what I want to know is, how did he come to tell me just at this time? Do you know?"

And then Merwin deemed that it was time to tell her all, so she made a clean breast of it, and Peggy was amazed to learn that Merwin had known the truth all along, as also had Dr. Scott and old Captain Wareham.

"But Daddy didn't tell Mr. Tate a thing about your secret under the figurehead, so that's all our own yet,"

THE FIRST RESULTS

Merwin ended, and Peggy felt more content with this knowledge. The whole incident had the effect of clearing the atmosphere in a very marked fashion, and from that time on, Peggy seemed happier and more cheerful than Merwin had yet seen her.

That afternoon Dr. Scott, instead of going off on his usual fishing expedition, proposed to Merwin and Peggy that they take a tramp down the beach with him and show him old Jonas's hut. He said they might even go farther if they had time, to the spot where the girls and Jim McLeod had found the trunk.

"Perhaps we haven't exhausted the possibilities of those two places yet," he said. "There's something I'm particularly looking for, and I have an idea we may come across it in one of those two places."

"What is it?" they both demanded in a breath. But he only answered:

"I'll tell you when the time comes. Bring that old fish line of mine along, Merwin—the one I decided yesterday to discard. It may come in handy. And we might carry the little hatchet, too. I don't think the ax is necessary now, since Jim obligingly cut a path through the jungle the other day."

They set off in high spirits. Merwin was perfectly happy at having her father with her. Now that he had been admitted to the mystery, it seemed more like a glorious adventure and less like the sad oppressive secret that it had been before. And Peggy confided to her that it was a great deal more fun to have Dr. Scott along with them.

The doctor was indeed a man whose personality held a special appeal for children and young people, and they never failed to respond to it because they realized instinctively that he understood them.

When they reached Jonas's hut, the doctor advised caution about entering it, for their program did not include a brush with a wildcat defending her young. So after making a sufficient racket to disturb her if she happened to be within and obtaining no results, they decided to enter boldly, especially as there were no tracks or footprints about to indicate a recent entry or exit.

Rather to the surprise of the girls, they found even the kittens gone from the nest where they had first discovered the little creatures, and there were no traces of the fierce youngsters anywhere in the vicinity. But the doctor explained that undoubtedly the wildcat had removed them to parts unknown, for she easily detected that strange humans had been about the premises. And like all wild animals, she had been unwilling to continue in a retreat that had been invaded by enemies.

The coast thus clear, they proceeded to reinvestigate the interior of the tumbledown shack. And the doctor, whom Merwin now laughingly dubbed "Detective," insisted on a close scrutiny of every article in the conglomerate heap on the floor and as close a one of the contents of the bedroom.

"If you only had a magnifying glass, you'd be the perfect image of a real detective!" she teased. And he replied that he wished he *had* brought one, though what he was

THE FIRST RESULTS

looking for would doubtless be visible without its aid. And when they again besought him for an explanation, he countered that since they were pleased to call him "Detective," he was going to be just as mysterious as he wanted to be and give them no satisfaction till he had found what he was searching for—if he ever did find it.

Finally, he turned the two girls out of the hut and came out himself.

"There's absolutely nothing more to be found here unless we dig up under the floor," he asserted, "and I'm not prepared to do that today. Anyway, as I figure it, Jonas never kept in that place anything he really wanted to hide except the old map which he intended for Jim McCleod. He wouldn't have thought his secrets safe in the hut, I imagine. Now let's proceed on down to the tunnel. I think there's time to give that a look-over before we have to return."

They tramped on down the beach, the doctor asking them innumerable questions about little side issues of the mystery into which Merwin had not had time or had not thought to go during her account of it to him the day before. And before they realized it, they had come to the old wreck by the dunes indicated in Jonas's crude map. And then they plunged into the tunnel through the mass of wreckage beyond, the two girls reveling in the very obvious surprise of Dr. Scott at this curious survival of old Jonas's secret hiding place.

"I've understood that there used to be a rumor to the effect that he had a secret lair somewhere in this muddle," he said, "but no one has ever succeeded in finding it. You could hunt for years, literally, in this wilderness of wreckage and undergrowth without ever coming within miles of this particular spot. Jonas certainly chose well."

As all three could not conveniently fit into the tiny shack and leave room for any exploration, the two girls remained outside and left the doctor to examine minutely the meager contents of the shelter and the old trunk. But from the doorway they watched with keen interest, and presently Merwin was called in to hold the big electric torch he had brought along while he scrutinized, tapped, and prodded at the bottom of the trunk.

"I was thinking it might have a false bottom," he told them, "or possibly something might be concealed in the lining. But this old paper lining has peeled off or fallen off almost completely, from the dampness, and the bottom of the trunk is rotting away. So I guess we're left, as far as that goes. Here, just take hold of it on that end and help me move it. It's empty, so it won't be heavy."

He and Merwin grasped the trunk, each by one of its iron handles at the side. To Merwin's amazement, however, they could not budge it.

"Whatever is the matter?" she gasped, staring incredulously at it. The doctor only smiled.

"I discovered that when I was tapping around it," he said, "but I thought I'd let you girls have the fun of finding it out for yourselves. It's nailed to the floor."

"But why?" demanded the girls in chorus.

"That's what we're going to find out," he answered and

THE FIRST RESULTS

began to pry at the bottom of the trunk with the hatchet.

It was some time before he succeeded in prying it loose from the boards of the flooring to which it had been nailed with many long and stout nails. And when he did at last get it loose from its moorings, it was to the almost complete destruction of the bottom of the trunk.

"Never mind!" he laughed. "It wasn't worth preserving anyway. And now we can see what this little practical joke of old Jonas's is all about."

The flooring under the trunk bore the look of having been tampered with many times. The boards had been sawed across in two or three places and were obviously fitted into their places without the use of nails to hold them down. The blade of the hatchet, used as a wedge, easily pried one up, and two more were pulled out without any effort. And underneath, lying in a hollow dug out of the sand and lined with rotting sailcloth, was a curious collection of articles. And at the sight of them, the doctor gave a pleased chuckle.

"Just as I thought!" he exclaimed, gathering them up and laying them out on the floor. "I had a notion he'd be likely to hide them somewhere."

"What is it? What is it?" clamored Merwin and Peggy, bending over him to examine the find. But just at that moment, the trio were startled by a sharp flash and a loud report that brought them all to their feet with a jump.

"A heavy thunderstorm," remarked the doctor. "I saw it gathering as we came along the beach. But I knew we couldn't get back to the hotel before it broke, so might as well be in this shelter as any. We'll probably get something of a setting, anyhow, as the roof's pretty much of a sieve, but at least it's better than being out in the open. Here comes the rain."

A blackness as of night had shut down on the tiny shack, and sheets of rain began to descend on the inadequate roof, streaming in through its many holes. A spot in one corner proved the only comparatively dry one, and in this they all huddled, the doctor having first scrambled together their find and wrapped it up in the old sailcloth, tied with the fish line Merwin had brought at his request. It made rather a bulky parcel.

So like a deluge was the downpour, and so sharp and persistent the lightning and thunder, that for a time they had no thought of anything save their efforts to keep dry and safe from the storm. And when it was over at last, the doctor, looking at his watch by the light of the electric torch, announced that it was much later than he had thought and that they would barely have time to get home to supper if they put on full steam.

So they left the shack, he carrying the parcel containing their new find. And all the satisfaction they could get from him, concerning its nature, was the assurance that he'd show them all about it next morning if they wouldn't ask any more questions just then.

CHAPTER XV

Several New Developments

THE NEXT MORNING dawned clear and cold. A biting northwest wind raced over the tumbled waters of the bay but flattened down the ocean surf till it was little more than a feeble wash. At breakfast, Billy proposed to the doctor a deep-sea fishing expedition, and Merwin fairly held her breath in suspense till she heard her father reply that he had some rather important work to attend to that morning and didn't think he'd better go off for even part of the day. Billy looked surprised and somewhat grieved at this response to his invitation and evidently was at a loss to understand the doctor's lack of enthusiasm. But as his guests' wishes were law, no matter how singular their foibles might be, Billy was obliged to let it go at that.

"Get Peggy and come to my room a little later," the doctor whispered to Merwin, "and we'll see what we can make of the latest development in this riddle." Needless to say, Merwin and Peggy were on hand betimes, and they found Dr. Scott spreading out across the expanse of his bed the collection from the old sailcloth.

"Well, *will* you tell us *now* what all this strange lot of junk means?" queried Merwin, eyeing the assortment of bits of wood that lay in a conglomerate mass on the counterpane. "I can't imagine what they are, and Peggy and I are going just about crazy to find out."

"All right," grinned the doctor, his long, clever, capable surgeon's fingers arranging and rearranging the articles in some inexplicable pattern. "This is a little picture-puzzle of old Jonas's that he was kind enough to prepare for our diversion. If the old man had lived a little later, he might have fixed it in the form of a modern crossword puzzle. All joking aside, though, can't you see what has happened to these pieces of wood? Just examine them closely and see what you make of them yourselves."

Merwin and Peggy both bent over the curious little blocks of wood, none of them more than three inches in diameter and all rather irregular in shape and size. They had been painted on one side, and the edges showed plain traces of having been cut roughly with a saw. The painted sides were black, with here and there the faint traces of tarnished gilt.

"I know!" cried Peggy suddenly. "They were all one piece of wood once and have been sawed up into these little pieces. Is that right, Dr. Scott?"

"Exactly; only I'm not sure whether it was one or two pieces they were in. But they have been sawed up, and our problem now is to get them together so that they'll make the one or two pieces they originally were."

"But why?" demanded Merwin. "What good would it do if we do get them pieced together as they were?"

"I thought I'd given you the hint when I said it was old Jonas's little picture-puzzle," went on the doctor. "But if you can't guess—and, after all, you hardly would—I'll tell you what I think it is. Do you remember the wreck that Dr. Trenway told you about?—the one that was washed ashore intact up on the dunes near old Jonas's hut? Well, he said that wreck was minus everything that could possibly identify it, even its name boards having been torn away. That gave me an idea. It seemed to me quite likely that this had been the work of someone on shore, for while a ship might conceivably be without any crew or passengers (they might have been washed overboard or drowned in trying to escape in a small boat, and it's also likely her captain or officers might have taken her log book and papers with them and those also have been lost), it isn't conceivable that anyone aboard her would have wrenched off her name from stern or prow. That would be a wholly senseless and ridiculous proceeding, wouldn't it?"

The girls nodded.

"Then this could only be the work of someone on shore who had some reason for wanting the ship's identity to remain unknown. If old Jonas had had an opportunity to go through her before anyone else discovered her whereabouts (and it's altogether likely, since she was cast up right at his door) and came upon anything in her of value that he wanted to conceal, he'd undoubtedly make every effort to keep her identity unknown. And the best way to do it would be to destroy her name. She might be traced, were her name made public, and that might have been bad for him."

"I see what you mean," suddenly interjected Merwin. "You think these pieces of wood are the boards on which that name was, and that if we get them together right we'll find out the name. But, Daddy, what I can't understand is this: Why didn't Jonas really destroy the boards if he wanted to hide the thing? Why did he keep them and saw them all up like this? There doesn't seem any sense to it. Surely it would have been safer to burn the whole thing, wouldn't it?"

"It certainly would," assented the doctor, "but here's where you've got to take into consideration old Jonas's peculiar mental makeup. He's a strange psychological study. I can only explain it by saying he had the *hoarding mania*. A good many people have it more or less mildly, but he had it in its most virulent form. In fact, I think we could almost say he was insane on the subject. He never threw *anything* away or destroyed anything. The condition of his own hut proclaims that fact. I recognized the type just from your description of the state of things there and felt pretty sure that somewhere or other he had hidden those name boards, though I confess I didn't expect to find them in the shape they are. Jonas evidently didn't dare to keep them so that they could be read, so he sawed them all up, as you see. But he wasn't going to throw them away—not he—and he concealed all the fragments. Perhaps he was just following his bent for hoarding; perhaps he wanted them for future reference. Who can tell?"

"Well, let's get right to work, then, and see if we can put these together!" cried Merwin, now all enthusiasm. "It's as good as a game. Makes me think of the picture-puzzles I used to play with when I was a tiny little thing." And she and Peggy fell to work with keen zest.

All morning the three labored over the puzzle, the doctor as keen as the others to work it out and decidedly quicker in piecing together the ragged edges of those uneven blocks. Their problem was increased by the fact that the gilt of the letters was so tarnished and rubbed as to be quite indistinguishable in places. But by noon they had most of the pieces fitted into what seemed their respective places and the whole puzzle so far yielded the following results:

L BEL DENIS

MA SEI LES

"Well, I can't make a thing out of that, can you?" sighed Merwin ruefully, surveying their work when the dinner bell rang, calling them away to other interests. "The letters that are rubbed out and the pieces that don't seem to fit are just enough to spoil it all."

The doctor, who had been for some time past sitting at the window, going over the old letter and diary, rather than paying any attention to the matter in hand, laughed somewhat unfeelingly.

"I gave it up some time ago because I'd got all I wanted

to out of it without digging over the thing any more. And I wanted a few quiet moments to study over this part of the problem, so I left you two to finish out the work if you could."

"Then what do you make it out to be?" they demanded, falling upon him for an instant explanation.

"We can pretty easily figure that out now as 'La Belle Denise, Marseilles,'" he answered, pointing out to them the way in which the missing letters would fill in the vacant spaces. "And down here in the corner are two figures, 'eighty-two,' which undoubtedly stand for 'eighteen-twenty' something or other, meaning that the vessel was built in the eighteen-twenties. That gives us a date near enough to work on in case I try to make any inquiries about this vessel. I think we've done a pretty good morning's work, on the whole, so let's celebrate by going down to dinner."

After dinner the two girls demanded what was to come next, and Merwin begged to be let off from her daily nap in order that not a moment of precious time should be wasted, now that they were so clearly upon the right track.

"How's it going to help you, now that you have the name of that vessel?" she demanded of her father. "I don't see that it tells us a thing about the rest of the mystery."

"It has given me several hints already," he declared, "and I felt so sure that we could find it that I wanted to nail that down before we did anything else. But now I'm going off on another track, and I think you and Peggy had better come with me out to the old figurehead and we'll continue our investigations there. But I want you to take that nap first because your health is of paramount importance to me, mystery or no mystery; and while you're taking it, I'm going up the beach to have a visit with old Captain Wareham and see if I can't get a little information from him, without giving away Peggy's secret. You and Peggy can meet me in a couple of hours down by the figurehead, and we'll continue investigations there."

The doctor appeared later in the afternoon with a decidedly pleased expression in his eyes. The two girls were sitting in front of the figurehead, gazing out to sea, when he came trudging down the beach. So absorbed was he in what he had to tell that he did not notice the very sober and rather alarmed expression on the faces of both girls but plunged at once into what he had to say.

"The old captain certainly has a long memory!" he chuckled. "He can go back farther than anyone I know, even old Dr. Trenway, when it comes to things that happened on this beach. I got him to talking about that old wreck of Jonas's, of course without giving away any of our discoveries about it. He saw it while it lay here for those seven or eight months so many years ago. Of course, he was only a boy himself, and there weren't any life-saving stations or coast guards in those days. But he told me that the wreck was a nine-days' wonder in this neighborhood and that a number of people came over from the mainland to visit it. He himself was only a boy, but he remembers making an expedition over here with some cronies of his, rowing across the bay to spend a day exploring the wreck. They very wisely waited around unobserved till they saw old Jonas go off up the beach and then bolted into the wreck and spent a happy day rummaging around in its water-logged interior.

"He says there isn't much that escaped their eyes that day, and he found something in the ship that even old Jonas had overlooked, apparently. It was tucked down behind a berth in one of the cabins, doubtless one that had been occupied by a passenger, if there were any passengers on that voyage. He said he had always kept it as one of his sea curiosities—and he has a large collection of such in his room at the station. I persuaded him to let me take it with me to examine more closely, and here it is."

He drew something from his pocket and handed it to the girls, saying as he did so:

"This is one of the most valuable clues we've struck so far."

"Oh, it's a book!" exclaimed Merwin. "A little old book! And it looks as if it had been well soaked in water, too. And it's all in French. Let's see if I can translate what it says . . . 'Fables of La Fontaine' . . . why, Dad, we read those in school! But what's that got to do with our mystery, and how is it going to help us?"

"Look on the flyleaf," was his reply, and she turned to the flyleaf at once.

"There's writing here," she responded, "but it's awfully faint and blurred—the water, I suppose. Can you read what it says, Dad? I can't make it out."

"Yes, I can read it, and it's a most important three

lines of writing, as you'll see. It says—I'll translate into English—'To my dear little friend, David R., from Lucien Charles, Prince Murat, Bordentown, eighteen-thirty-two.'"

"But Dad, what does it all mean? What can it have to do with the puzzle we're interested in? I don't understand."

"It has so much to do with it that I'm pretty sure it's going to help us clear the whole thing up. But it's necessary to go a little into history in order to explain it to you, and I don't want to take the time to do that just now. I mean to do a little investigating right around here, just at present, and tonight I'll explain to you about this book. But what are you two youngsters looking so solemn about?" For at the mention of their present locality, the faces of the girls had suddenly grown very serious.

"There's something strange here, Dr. Scott," declared Peggy. "We discovered it as soon as we got here this afternoon. Come around to the back and we'll show you."

They all moved round to the back of the figurehead, and Peggy pointed to the sand at its foot.

"This must have been done since last evening's storm," she said, "'cause the sand was all smoothed out then."

And looking down, Dr. Scott saw that the sand at the foot of the statue was deeply indented with large footprints.

CHAPTER XVI

A Meddler in the Mystery

"H M! I DON'T like the looks of this so very much!" exclaimed the doctor, bending down to examine the marks. They were particularly thick directly at the base of the figurehead's pedestal and it also appeared as if someone had been digging in the sand around, although there seemed to be no reason to think the effort had amounted to much more than some futile poking and prodding with a stick.

"Where do those footprints lead from . . . or to?" he presently asked, walking around to the front to ascertain.

A trail of them appeared to lead from the direction of the beach toward the south, as if someone had come up from that direction. But they did not return that way, appearing rather to point down toward the bay for a few steps, where they were thereafter lost in the rank grass and bushes.

"Somebody's been snooping around here, but for what purpose it would be rather hard to say. It may not have anything to do with our affairs, and yet, again, what possible reason would one have for poking about here, if it were not connected with that? The only person whom we might have the slightest reason to suspect would be Jim McCleod. By the way, girls, does he know anything about this part of the mystery?"

"Not a thing," declared Merwin. "We never mentioned anything to him about the figurehead or what Peggy found, or a single word about any other part of it. And that afternoon, when we were leaving old Jonas's hiding place, we made him solemnly promise that he'd never tell a living soul anything about what he knew because it was our secret—we'd found it first—and we didn't want anyone else prying into it. He did promise, and I'm certain he'd keep a promise. He seems an awfully trustworthy sort of boy."

"Besides," asserted Peggy, "these aren't Jim's footprints. They're a good deal larger than the shoe he wears, broader; Jim's foot is rather narrow. He says the fellows are always teasing him at the station and telling him he has a woman's foot."

"True enough," agreed the doctor, bending to examine the footprints again. "They belong to a bigger man; I should say they *did*. I have the average-sized foot for a man, and my feet are lost in them." He put his own foot inside one of the prints, and the edges of his soles came an inch inside of the print all the way around. "Now, who in conscience around here has a foot like that?"

"'Tisn't Grandpa," decided Peggy. "His foot is quite a different shape. I've often noticed the print of his boots, and they're nothing like that. And Mr. Dillon and Mr. Presby went home yesterday morning, so they couldn't have been here. There's only the station folks left, unless it's some stranger over from the mainland that we didn't see."

"That's not very likely," declared the doctor, "at this time of year. No, I guess we've simmered it down to the station. I'll take notice, next time I'm there, and see who has such enormous feet. Meantime, all we can do is to keep an eye on this place and see if we can catch anyone fooling around it. I'd rather hate to think that anyone has gotten wind of this business before we have a chance to clear up the mystery. Peggy and Merwin, you two keep watch in all directions and see that no one is spying on us while I do a little digging down here. I want to get an idea whether or not there could possibly be anything under there that we haven't unearthed yet. Where's that old trowel you always use?"

Peggy found it for him in the old shack, and he went to work with it while the two girls perched at the front of the figurehead, their eyes sweeping the horizon in every direction. But the beach appeared that day to be deserted. Only Billy Tate's fat figure, waddling out to the dock to get something from his motor boat moored there, presented itself for five minutes and then disappeared into the hotel. At length the doctor desisted from his hopeless efforts to make a wider opening into the interior of the platform.

"I simply can't make any impression on it with this little trowel," he declared. "It needs a good, wide spade. The sand just shifts down into that hole as fast as I get it dug out. Can't get my head down far enough to see into it, either. Guess we'll have to try this again under more scientific or workmanlike conditions. I'm going back to the hotel now to study up a little more on the clue I got from the old captain. After all, that's the most important thing we've struck so far."

The girls spent the rest of the afternoon in a little crabbing expedition on the bay. Crabbing always fascinated Merwin, and for a time she forgot the mystery in her absorption in scooping up immense green and blue grandfather crabs from the end of the dock while Peggy lured them near with a fish head tied to a piece of a string. When the girls had a peach basket full of crabs, they took them up to Mrs. Tate, who promised to boil them that night. But she said the girls must pick the meat out without fail next morning, if she cooked them, for she wasn't going to have them lie around and spoil. Otherwise she was going to throw them all back in the bay. The girls gave their solemn promise to do this, little realizing what bearing all this was to have on matters far more important to their minds.

That same night, directly after supper, Billy Tate announced that he was going to build a big fire down on the beach—something he had long been promising Peggy that he would do—and that they were all invited down to roast apples and toast marshmallows. The experience was a new one to Merwin and a very delightful one. She and Peggy forgot their momentary disappointment that they could not devote the evening to talking over the mystery with Dr. Scott and thoroughly enjoyed sitting around

Never was there more of a nightmare ordeal than that experienced by the chilled, half-fainting, wholly terror-stricken girl sunk to her armpits in the deceitful quicksand, with night closing in about her and the prospect of rescue, before she grew too faint to maintain her hold, growing more uncertain with every passing moment. She tried to close her eyes and forget where she was and pretend that she was safely back in the hotel in her warm bed, but the effort was useless. She tried to think of her father and summon up courage such as she knew would be in him in similar circumstances. She could almost hear him say: "Keep a stiff upper lip, Merwin. Buck up, little girl. It's going to be all right." Only the thought of him nerved her to renewed effort to conquer the terrible faintness and maintain her hold on the spar.

It was after an eternity of waiting that she heard Peggy's voice shouting from the dune top:

"Oh, Merwin! Hang on! We're coming. It's all right. I've got Jim with me."

Merwin did hang on, but it must have been in a semi-conscious condition, for she could never remember afterward any details of her rescue—anything, in fact, after that shout of Peggy's, till she found herself, hours later, wrapped in hot blankets in her bed at the hotel, and her father gently trying to force a spoonful of something into her mouth.

"Don't talk, dear!" he ordered. "I know you're crazy to hear how you got out of there, so while you drink this broth I'll tell you, but you mustn't try to say a word. Peggy and Jim McCleod, the Coast Guard patrol, managed to pry you out somehow—I'll never understand how they did it!—and they carried you, between them, halfway back here. Then, as both were almost exhausted, they wrapped you in a coat and sweater and Peggy stayed with you where you lay on the beach, while Jim came down here and got us all out. I had just returned from fishing and was anxious enough about you.... But let's not think of it any more. You had a narrow escape, little girl, and you owe your life to Peggy. Now, go to sleep."

A little later, in the next room, the doctor had a rather curious interview with Peggy, whom he had also sent to bed, as she was chilled and exhausted and terribly overwrought nervously after her recent experience. He had entered the room with some medicine in a glass and, sitting beside the bed, had bidden her sip it slowly. Then, as he took the glass from her, he said, laying his free hand over her cold little ones:

"How am I ever going to thank you, Peggy, for saving my little girl's life?" But curiously enough, Peggy started up at this and stared at him with big and anxious gray eyes.

"I don't deserve any thanks, Doctor! Please... please don't try to thank me! I didn't do right. I got to tell you now ... or I'll go crazy. I wasn't nice to Merwin ... I wouldn't talk to her or ... or be with her ... or anything. I forgot my promise to you ... and I let her go off by herself ... today. If I'd gone with her she wouldn't have got into this. Oh, I can't forgive myself ... and you won't forgive me, either, I know!" She fell back and buried her face in the pillow and sobbed hysterically.

But the doctor only patted her shoulder understandingly.

"Don't, little Peggy!" he soothed. "I understand perfectly. She was too strange. You couldn't get used to her at first. But she's pure gold—my little girl—and so are you. You've got to be friends, after this. Promise me?"

Again Peggy looked up into his kind brown eyes, with her tear-wet ones, and promised. And this time she meant to keep her promise.

CHAPTER V

In Which Peggy Redeems Her Promise

BY HER FATHER'S orders, Merwin remained in bed two days. Besides the cold and exposure, she had experienced a severe mental shock in her terrible experience, and for twenty-four hours Dr. Scott almost feared that it might permanently affect her. But on the second morning she seemed more like her old, cheerful self and pleaded to see Peggy, if that elusive little lady could be induced to enter the room. And deeming company of her own age the best tonic for her, the doctor gave his consent and went to hunt Peggy up.

Peggy now needed little urging to go and keep Merwin company. Truth to tell, she had been longing for this opportunity all of the day before, but she was far too shy to ask it. She went with Dr. Scott willingly, and he left the two girls together, only warning them laughingly not to talk themselves to death.

It was Merwin who broke through the slight constraint

that was inevitable when they were at last alone.

"Don't let's talk of what's happened, Peggy," she began. "I can't bear even to think of it. I dream of it every minute when I'm asleep and think I'm disappearing completely into that horrible place. Oh!..." She shuddered and hid her face in her hands.

"No, we won't talk of it," responded Peggy hurriedly. "I know just how you feel. I want to talk to you about some other things—something I never thought I'd talk to anyone about." She was summoning all her wits to the work of distracting Merwin from the thoughts of her recent nightmare. For, on their way to Merwin's room, Dr. Scott had made this urgent demand of her.

"There's something I want to beg you to try to do, Peggy," he whispered. "Merwin simply *must* be made to forget her awful experience somehow. I'm almost afraid it may affect her mind if she doesn't stop thinking about it. Try to interest her in something else. Try to distract her thoughts if you possibly can. I think you can do this better than anyone else. Will you do this thing for me, Peggy?"

And in the moment that she had given him her word, she had made a compact with herself. Perhaps there *was* something she knew that would serve the purpose; she felt almost sure of it. And, although it was her own deepest secret, the thing she had firmly resolved never to tell anybody, she was willing to impart it now if it would help to remedy a condition that she realized was in some measure due to her own failure to keep her promise.

While she was trying to think of the best method of

IN WHICH PEGGY REDEEMS HER PROMISE

opening the subject, Merwin asked her if she had read any of the book and how she liked it.

"Oh, I've finished it!" cried Peggy, relieved at this opening. "I thought . . . it was *wonderful*! I've never read a mystery story before. I . . . well, I just can't stop thinking about it."

Merwin laughed.

"It was good, but I've read better ones than that, even. I think I have some detective stories in my trunk. I must let you have them. *They're* the most wonderful detective and mystery stories I've ever read. You'll go crazy over *them*."

"Oh, I'd love to have them!" sighed Peggy, and then she was silent for a moment or two. It seemed very difficult, somehow, to introduce the subject she intended to talk about, although she had now the very opening she wanted. Presently she asked shyly: "Have you ever had a . . . a mystery in your . . . your own life?"

"Why, no!" exclaimed Merwin. "I've never had any such thing. Have you one, Peggy?"

"There's something," said Peggy, slowly. "It's hard to tell you just how it . . . it came about that I found it. But it's very strange. Sometimes it frightens me. I've . . . I've never found any answer to it. I don't know what it all means. No one knows about it except me. Not even Grandpa Tate, and I've always told him pretty nearly everything."

She stopped again, at a loss how to begin the revelation, but Merwin sensed her predicament and tried to help out.

"Has it anything to do with the . . . the figurehead?" she suggested. Peggy stared at her, with a little gasp.

"How did you know?" She faltered, eyeing Merwin with just a slight return of suspicion.

"I *don't* know anything ... and I haven't been spying on you, Peggy," Merwin hastened to reassure her. "But perhaps you don't realize that you acted rather strangely about that place the very first day I came ... when I asked if it was hollow underneath and if one could get in there. I didn't mean anything at all by that question; I asked it more for the sake of saying something than any other reason. But you remember the way you took it?" Peggy nodded.

"Well, that set me to wondering, first of all. Then, next morning, quite by accident, I happened to see you digging under the place and pulling things out from it and hiding them again there. I suppose I oughtn't to have watched you, but I didn't realize quite that I was doing that till afterward. I hope you won't think I meant to do anything mean. And then, there was what you said the other day when I was sitting by the figurehead. It has all made me wonder very much, but I truly wasn't trying to pry into your secret, Peggy."

Reassured by Merwin's very genuine explanation, Peggy thawed, the chill of suspicion disappearing from her manner.

"I see how it was," she responded. "I didn't know I was ... giving myself away ... like that. But I honest-to-goodness thought you suspected something and was ... were trying to dig it out of me. I ... I almost hated you because you were a city girl and ... and ... oh, those girls were so horrid to me in Toms River!" And in her renewed feeling

IN WHICH PEGGY REDEEMS HER PROMISE

of confidence, she told Merwin all about her unhappy experience at school.

"So I felt's if I couldn't like girls very much after that. But, anyhow, this ain't telling you about the mystery. I don't hardly know how to begin about that, but it's like this: I always liked to play by that old figurehead, ever since I was as little as I can remember. And one time—it must have been four or five years ago—I was playing there one day, digging in the sand at the back and pretending I was a pirate and was going to bury my treasure. I'd collected a pile of pretty shells and stones that I really did think a lot of and was going to bury those somewhere down by the figurehead. So I dug and dug a deep hole in the sand right where there was a strange little mark on one of the boards, like a painted cross. I hadn't ever noticed that little mark before, and I thought it was good fun to pretend that mark was to show where I had a secret hiding place.

"Well, I got down pretty deep, and I came to a hole in one of those big timbers, as if it had been sawed away there sometime or other. I thought that was kind of strange because the next one to it didn't seem like that at all. So I reached down and put my hand into the hole . . . what do you think I found?"

Merwin had been listening, absorbed, to the recital, her own troubles completely forgotten.

"I can't imagine!" she breathed. "What was it, Peggy?"

"It was . . . a strange thing," answered Peggy. "I could feel it, but I couldn't see it because I couldn't get my head down near enough to the hole. The sand would come tumbling back and get in the way. I tried, but even when I got my head there for a minute it shut out the light, and I couldn't see anyway. You see, the hole was pretty far down. Well, anyhow, I reached in my hand and pulled it out. And it was..."

She paused dramatically, and Merwin half raised herself in bed in the intensity of her excitement and interest.

"It was... a curious little box... about so big." She indicated with her hands something about ten inches long, not quite so wide, and three or four inches high. "It came open—the lid was on a hinge—and you'll never guess what it was!"

"No, I can't!" cried Merwin. "Tell me, quick, Peggy!"

"It was a work box or sewing box. It had papers of needles and spools of thread and silk and a thimble and pieces of different kinds of cloth—little pieces—and one tiny dress, a baby's dress, I think, though it looked hardly bigger than a doll's. It was only partly finished. Wasn't that a strange thing to find in there?"

"Awfully strange!" sighed Merwin breathlessly. "How in the world did it ever come there, and whose was it? Have you ever found out?"

"No, I haven't," acknowledged Peggy hesitantly. "I know it's nothing that ever belonged to Grandma Tate or anyone here because once I described the box to her in just a... a general sort of way—I didn't quite want to tell her my secret—and she said she'd never heard of one like

IN WHICH PEGGY REDEEMS HER PROMISE

that. You see, the box is strange anyway; different from any I'd ever seen. It's of wood, black wood of some kind, and metal corners sort of fancy or carved—maybe brass or silver, but they're so tarnished I can't tell which. And there's a carved handle on the cover. It has a lock, too, but no key. And when I first pulled it out, it wasn't locked but tied up in tarpaulin with pieces of cord. The cord was so rotten that it fell right off before I could untie it."

Merwin was by now so excited that she couldn't lie still in bed, but sat up with hands clasped about her knees.

"My gracious!" she exclaimed. "This is the most thrilling thing I've ever heard! But was that all that was in the box, Peggy?"

"No," Peggy answered, "it wasn't all, or even the most interesting part. I'm coming to that. There was an old letter and a little book, a book that you write in every day the things that happen. I don't know what you call it."

"A diary?" suggested Merwin.

"Yes, I guess that's it. It seemed to be that sort of thing."

"But, Peggy," cried Merwin, suddenly interrupting. "If you found things like *that*—a diary and a letter—I should think it would be quite easy to make out whom the box had belonged to and even, perhaps, how it came to be in such a strange place."

"Yes, you *would* think that," replied Peggy with an odd little smile, "but both were strange, very strange, and if you could see them, you wouldn't wonder that it didn't tell anything, only made things more strange."

"Why? Were they in some foreign language?"

"No, but you'd have to see them to understand what I mean."

"Oh, I *want* to see them right away!" exclaimed Merwin, falling back on her pillow and thumping it in her excitement. "I wonder if Daddy would let me get up right now—I'm *perfectly* well again—and go out to the figurehead with you."

"I don't hardly think he will," smiled Peggy. "He said you must stay in bed at least the rest of this day. But I'll go ask him if you like. He's sitting down on the veranda, reading. He told me I'd find him there if you needed him."

"Well, do go right away!" urged Merwin. "Tell him I just *must* get up! I feel fine. I'll go crazy staying in bed any longer."

Peggy went off on her errand, and Dr. Scott came back with her. He smiled at Merwin whimsically but was plainly well pleased that she seemed to have at last forgotten her terrible experience.

"So you want to get up and go out, honey?"

"Oh, yes, Dad! *Do* let me!" But Dr. Scott felt that she was not yet strong enough to be wandering around at large and said so very firmly.

"Just this one day more in bed, and then you can tramp around at your own sweet will. Aren't you having a good time with Peggy?"

"Wonderful!" she acknowledged, with a little grin of understanding at her new friend.

"Then stay here, both of you, and finish up the day," he commanded as he left the room. And the two girls knew it was useless to argue the matter any further.

"Never mind. You can tell me some more about that strange box," sighed Merwin as she settled herself back with as much resignation as she could muster. "What else was there in it that was strange, Peggy?"

"There was nothing else much. The strangeness was mostly in that letter and diary. When you see them you'll understand—"

But here Merwin interrupted with another idea:

"Peggy, if there was a letter, it must have had some address on the envelope. Wouldn't that give you an idea about anything?"

"There wasn't any envelope. It must have been torn off or lost before the letter was ever put in there."

"Well, that's too bad. But surely, Peggy, there *must* have been something in that box to give you some sort of clue! And there's another thing: you said at first that there was something about this mystery that frightened you. I can't understand what you mean by that. Why should it frighten you to have discovered this thing? It's curious, I'll admit, and very puzzling. But why is there anything about it to alarm *you*?"

"Because," said Peggy in a very low voice, "it seemed ... I can't tell you how just yet ... but it seemed to have something to do ... with *me!*"

CHAPTER VI

The Heart of the Mystery

THE NEXT MORNING Merwin was up and about early, showing no ill effects of her recent harrowing experience. In fact, so full of excitement was she that Dr. Scott wondered what had come over her.

"Want to go down the beach fishing with me this morning?" he suggested and was astonished to have his usually appreciated invitation turned down with scarcely an apology.

"I've an engagement with Peggy this morning, thanks!" laughed Merwin. "You won't mind if I go off with her?" The doctor was only too well pleased to have her in the company of someone her own age, and he gave Peggy an approving smile when he passed her later on his way out to fish.

"You've done it, Peggy. Congratulations!" was all he said, but Peggy flushed to the roots of her bronze hair with pleasure at his brief words of praise. Ten minutes later the girls were scrambling hotfoot through the fragrant bay bushes to the pedestal of the old figurehead.

When they knelt in the sand at its base, Peggy with the old trowel in her hand, Merwin pointed to the little cross and remarked:

"You tried to get that off the day I saw you, didn't you, Peggy?"

"Yes, I did," she acknowledged, turning red again. "I thought you might discover it and . . . and suspect everything. I tried to scrape it off, but it wouldn't go. . . . Forgive me, won't you?"

Merwin only squeezed her hand in reply, and the digging began in earnest. It seemed to Merwin as if she could scarcely wait for the requisite hole to be dug and the strange opening to appear. And her mystification was even deeper than Peggy's because, after her revelation of the day before that the thing in some way concerned *her*, Peggy had refused to go any further till she could introduce Merwin to the very heart of the puzzle itself. She said it was too hard to explain unless Merwin could see for herself.

When at last the mysterious wooden box was laid in her lap, she experienced the sensation of unreality one has in a dream when impossible and unattainable treasures are at last within one's grasp. She fingered the tiny baby dress, yellowed and frail from exposure to dampness, and marveled over the fine hand-laid tucks and delicate lace, the unfinished buttonholes and hem. "What darling child could this have been for?" she wondered as she laid it aside and surveyed the spools of thread, the dainty, faded needlebook of pink satin, the gold thimble, and other articles of some fastidious woman's sewing gear. At last she turned to the letter and diary, which had been on top, and which Peggy had taken out first and held in her own lap.

"May I see those now?" she asked, and Peggy handed them to her, requesting only that she read the letter first. Opening it with fingers that actually trembled, she smoothed out its folds, exclaiming, as she did so, at the beautiful evenness and fineness of the writing. It had evidently been very much read and fingered, and the folds were almost worn through. Merwin remarked on this to Peggy, who said that it was already in that condition when she found it.

Dear friend (Merwin read aloud):

After a long and arduous search, I have at last located the J.B. treasure. Old Jonas Tow is dead and in his dying moments confessed to me where he had concealed it. I was not wrong, then, in suspecting that he knew—had always known—and I dogged him to the last, never allowing him a day's respite till he revealed it all to me when the end was near and he was in fear of death.

I think it would be best if you could come up here as soon as possible with the child. Since there is a reason why coming on one of the regular steamers would be difficult at present, I think I can arrange for you to take the trip in a slow way on some sailing vessel. It is slower that way but not at all an unpleasant trip. I happen to know very well the captain of one of those

Puerto Rican sailing vessels and will try to make arrangements with him to take you on his next trip north. If I succeed, I will cable you.

God willing, the end of your long struggle is at hand, and the time has arrived when you may rightfully come into your own.

Your faithful friend and servitor,

T.G.

When Merwin had finished reading this curious missive, she laid it in her lap and sat and stared at Peggy for several seconds in the complete silence of amazement. Then at last she drew in a long breath and spoke softly:

"What an adventure for you!"

"What do you mean?" asked Peggy, rather surprised at this comment.

"Why, that you should have stumbled on a mystery like this! It actually doesn't sound as if it could be real! I want to pinch myself to see that I'm not just dreaming—or reading a detective story.... Tell me more about this wonderful thing. Who wrote it, and to whom was it written?"

"That I don't know now any more than the day I found it," sighed Peggy. "It has no name on it, you see, only those initials and the 'Dear Friend.' How is anyone going to tell anything about it?"

"'The J.B. treasure.' Doesn't that sound just perfectly marvelous!" continued Merwin, glancing over it. "What can it be and where can it be? And who is Jonas Tow? *There's* a name for you, at least."

"Yes, but it doesn't help a bit."

"It might help a great deal in finding out what all this

is about. It's something, at least, to start from—a clue, as the detectives would call it. But anyway, Peggy, this isn't all there was. What's in that little diary you spoke about?"

Peggy slowly handed her over the little red-leather-covered book.

"There isn't much in it," she said. "You see, it began the first of January and only has two or three weeks filled in. Then . . . it's blank. After you read it, you can guess what happened. But it has in it the strangest thing of all."

It took a long while for Merwin to decipher the record. Seawater and salt dampness had blurred the writing, and the ink had faded in the years of concealment in its strange hiding place. Each page was the record of a day, and often there were abbreviations and references that meant nothing to her. But out of it all she gathered the daily life of someone on shipboard—some woman, plainly—and one unaccustomed to the sea and the rough life of a coastwise sailing ship. There were many references to storms and contrary winds, but the record consisted mainly of details concerning the welfare and the progress of a small baby that she evidently had with her. There were a number of entries similar to the following:

January 3. A terrific northeast gale today. The vessel is rolling horribly. I was extremely seasick this morning, but got over it. Tiny Margaret never seems to be. I began another little dress for her this afternoon, but it is hard to sew. Have to stay in the cabin, which is very stuffy, and I tied Baby in her berth, or she would have rolled out. I wish it had not been necessary to take the trip in this way. A regular steamer would have been so much quicker and more comfortable. Must turn in now and try to sleep, though I fancy there won't be much sleep tonight.

Toward the end there seemed to have been several days of fair weather without much wind, but the last entry told a tale that was very suggestive:

January 29. A most terrible storm all day, which is unfortunate, for we are off the Jersey coast, not far, I gather, from the very place they are to land Baby and me. The captain came to me this morning and told me to get my things together and he'd do his best when we came in sight of Barnegat Light. But if it was too bad he'd have to go on and take us to New York. Said he couldn't wait around, as he was already very late with the cargo he'd contracted to deliver there by the middle of the month. And it was very dangerous, too, in this weather. I don't know what to do. That would upset all T.'s plans. The storm is now a hurricane. I can scarcely write. Even Baby Margaret is frightened and crying. There is an appalling noise on deck. I don't know—

And that was all. The record broke off with an abruptness that was startling. Merwin looked over at Peggy when she reached the last word with the brief question, "And then?"

"Then," said Peggy, very low, "there was a shipwreck. You can guess *that*, without much chance of a mistake. But, anyhow, I know for certain, and some other time I'll tell you why. Yes, there was an awful shipwreck that night. Do you see what year it was, by the diary?"

"It was nineteen hundred and six," said Merwin, referring to the little book.

"Well, there's a record of that storm and that wreck, in the books of the Coast Guard station. I looked it up once, and I know."

"And what happened?" breathed Merwin, too intent to notice the drawn look in Peggy's face as she revived this last drama of the sea.

"They were all lost ... every single one ... except ..."

"'Except'?" echoed Merwin. "Oh, do go on, Peggy! It's awful to keep me waiting like this."

"Except ... the *baby*!"

"The baby?" cried Merwin, staring at her incredulously. "How do you know?"

"The record just says, *Baby, girl, about six months, saved. No identification.*"

When Peggy had made this revelation, she continued to gaze at Merwin with a tense and tragic expression in her big gray eyes. But Merwin was still too absorbed in the story to notice her look.

"And what became of it afterward? Did you ever find out?" she questioned. "And what became of the 'J.B. treasure'? And how did that box come to be where it was?"

Peggy ignored the first query and in answer to the two others said she hadn't the least idea about the treasure and that she couldn't imagine how the box had come to be buried beneath the figurehead or how it had come to be taken off the ship at all. That was all part of the mystery.

"But didn't the Coast Guard record tell you anything else?" Merwin demanded. "What was the name of the vessel or ... or anything?"

"Not a thing. They never knew the name of the ship."

Merwin sat, chin in hands, thinking it all over, her eyes fixed on the pathetic relics in her lap. Suddenly a new idea occurred to her.

"Peggy, there's something else. I just happened to think. You told me yesterday that this ... this mystery frightened you somehow because it seemed to have something to do with you. How in the world can that be? I don't see the slightest connection."

"Can't you guess?" asked Peggy very quietly.

"No, certainly not."

"Well, I'll tell you, then. I think ... I can't be sure ... but I sort of suspect ... that baby was ... *myself*."

CHAPTER VII

Old Captain Wareham

THERE ARE NO words adequate to describe the expression on Merwin's face when Peggy made this astounding announcement. Sheer incredulity almost drove her into exclaiming: "Oh, but Peggy! That's simply impossible." And then, hard upon this impulse came the remembrance of what her father had told her, on the very day of their arrival, of the girl's origin. Peggy's suspicion might have some foundation after all.

But Merwin realized at once, beyond this, that she was herself now in a very difficult position. How was she to discuss this matter with Peggy without revealing what she knew and what she had been warned not to divulge to her companion? At any cost, that secret must be kept since Billy Tate wished it so. She must go very cautiously and guard her tongue as never before. There must be no slip. And to this end, she could only answer:

"Surely you must be mistaken, Peggy! How could such a thing be? What makes you think so?"

And then, for the first time, she noticed the tragic expression in the girl's eyes. With a little, despairing movement of her hands, Peggy answered:

"I wish I were mistaken! Oh, how I wish I were!"

And Merwin was keen enough to read, in that brief exclamation, the nature of Peggy's tragedy. She wished to be what she had always thought she was—Billy Tate's granddaughter—and not some nameless waif of the sea.

"But tell me why you think so at all," Merwin insisted. "You must have some awfully good reason for such a wild guess as that."

"I have," Peggy answered. "My name's Peggy, isn't it—really Margaret? Well, that baby's name was Margaret. Wait a minute." For she saw Merwin was about to interrupt. "I know you're going to say there are hundreds of Margarets in the world and that that's a poor reason. But there's something else. There is a tiny gold ring of mine that I found once among Grandma Tate's things. It's a baby's ring and is cut in one place where it had to be filed off because I got too big for it and my hand was very fat and it wouldn't come off by itself. I asked Grandma once why I was named Margaret, as there didn't seem to be any other Margarets in the family that I'd ever heard of. She was very busy at the time and only said, 'Well, that's the name that was on your ring, isn't it?' And then she suddenly caught herself and looked scared and said in a sort of confused way: 'Oh well, I think your mother liked the name. It's pretty. Now you run out and get me those clams—right off.'"

"But even *that* doesn't prove anything," objected Merwin.

"I know it, but wait. Look at this page in the diary." And Peggy shuffled the leaves till she found a certain entry. Merwin, looking over her shoulder, read:

January 8. A very calm day and hot. Scarcely a breeze, and we made very little progress. Today tiny Margaret managed to work her little gold ring off her finger and had it in her mouth when I caught her. She's teething and wants something hard to bite on, I presume. She had already made a dent in her name on it with her little first tooth. I must fasten it on her in some way so that she cannot get it off again.

"And my little ring," said Peggy, "has a dent right in the middle of the name."

It seemed all too convincing a proof. Yet even so, Merwin was determined not to admit it to Peggy—even to herself. "It certainly is a strange coincidence," she acknowledged, "but I think it's scarcely more than that. Dozens of babies are named Margaret and have it on their rings; and babies are apt to chew on those rings when they're teething. There must be some better proof than that, Peggy."

"There is," her companion assured her. "Here's another page in the diary." And she shuffled the leaves anew and read aloud:

January 13. A clear day but with strong headwinds. I sat on deck with Baby nearly all day and sewed and read. She is beginning to have a crop of beautiful bronze-colored ringlets. Her hair is much lighter than mine, hardly more than a red-gold now. But no doubt it will grow darker with time. I cut off a curl to save it. I wonder what the future holds for us both.

"You'll say that's no proof, either," asserted Peggy, when she had finished reading the entry, "and I know it isn't. It's just one more thing to make me sure. But this is the one that even you'll have to admit is the strangest of all." And she turned to still another page and read:

January 21. Heavy fog most of the day. We are close off the coast and made little or no progress. Baby and I spent the day in our cabin. I noticed that the little spot or birthmark in the middle of the back of her right hand is growing larger as she grows. When she was born it was no bigger than a pinhead. Now it is almost an eighth of an inch in diameter, a little brown round spot. I hope it will not grow large enough to be disfiguring when she gets older. At present it only seems cute and rather odd.

And in answer to Merwin's unspoken question when she had finished reading this, Peggy simply held out her right hand to be inspected. And there, in the center, was a little light brown spot about three-eighths of an inch in diameter, which Merwin had never happened to notice before.

"Can there be any doubt about it after that?" Peggy demanded.

And this time Merwin had no answer for her. There could be no doubt; she had to admit it. Nevertheless, loyalty to Billy Tate's wish made her struggle to seem not entirely convinced.

"It's certainly very strange, Peggy," she admitted after

a pause. "But even so, I wouldn't take it for granted till it can be proved beyond a doubt. Let's not think of that side of it just now. You're Mr. and Mrs. Tate's granddaughter. You always have been, as far as you know, and they love you dearly. Let's just try to think what this mystery is all about and not connect it with yourself at present. There's something very, very strange about it. To begin with, how in the world did the box come to be hidden in this strange place?"

So she tried to draw Peggy's thoughts away from the dangerous subject and little by little led her mind into other channels of speculation. Peggy recounted more details of her first finding of the box some years before.

"You remember I told you how it was all wrapped up in an old piece of tarpaulin," she reminded Merwin. "And how it was tied up with a bit of cord, but the cord was so rotten that it fell apart in my hands. I didn't know how to read or write at the time, and I was just crazy to find out what it said in the letter and book, but I wouldn't tell anyone about it 'cause I wanted it for my secret. Then Grandpa Tate said he was going to send me to Toms River to school, and I was glad to go because I'd learn to read. But I . . . I couldn't stand it there . . . after all and had to come back. But just a little while after that, Professor Hanbridge came here to stay several months, and he taught me all I know. I studied just as hard as I could, and it seemed as if I couldn't learn fast enough. Then, when I could read writing, I puzzled it all out. But it was a long while before I thought . . . what I just told you a little while ago."

"How can I thank you enough for letting me into this wonderful secret, Peggy! It was fine of you to share it with me!" cried Merwin. "I hope you'll never have any reason to regret it."

"I won't regret it," answered Peggy confidently. "I never intended to tell you and I don't think I would have if—"

But here she broke off hastily, not caring to turn Merwin's thoughts back to her recent gruesome experience. But the clatter of the big dinner bell back at the hotel proved a sufficient diversion. Hastily reentering the box and its contents under the figurehead, the two girls scampered back to the house.

It seemed useless for Merwin to try to take her customary nap that afternoon. Her mind was in such a commotion after the revelations of the morning that sleep had never been further from her. But as she lay trying to while away the allotted hour, her busy brain began to sort out and rearrange the astounding facts she had learned and also to outline some plan for working out the puzzle. She wished very much that Peggy would allow her to confide in her father, but this she felt at the outset it was useless to ask. No, the girl would doubtless insist that they share the secret with no one, and if her suspicions were well founded, as Merwin only too well knew them to be, she doubtless had excellent reasons for not wishing it known.

She put that question aside, then, and began to arrange in her mind the clues on which they had to work. There seemed a number, and yet, when she came to analyze them, they proved unavailing enough for present purposes at least. There was not a single name to go by except that of Jonas Tow, whoever he might have been—or still was. No, that couldn't be, because the letter said he had just died. Doubtless that letter had been written at least fifteen years before. Although it was undated, it must have coincided, in the main, with the diary. They must count Jonas Tow out for the present.

What else was there to build upon that was in any way available? She could think of nothing except the record in the Coast Guard station that Peggy had mentioned. That they kept such records Merwin knew because when her father had taken her through the station and shown her all the interesting working of its boats and mechanisms, she had seen, among other things, the books in the little office where the account of each day's doings are kept, dozens of volumes dating back many years. Peggy had evidently investigated this herself, but Merwin felt that she must see it with her own eyes and perhaps ask Old Captain Wareham, the head of this particular station— who had seemed so ready, even eager, to show and tell her everything—a few questions. She thought that perhaps she, better than Peggy, could put them without rousing anyone's suspicions.

To this end, then, she decided to go that very afternoon and ask the old captain if she might spend a little while looking over the records because they interested her. She felt sure that he would offer no objection as he had urged her to come in and make herself at home in the place whenever she felt so inclined.

"Your father's a fine man," he had said with his genial smile. "Yes, I love Doctor Scott—I ain't ashamed to say it—and a daughter of his'n is as welcome as a southwest breeze!" And her father had grinned at that and added:

"You'd better take the captain up on that offer, Merwin. He can tell you many a grand, hair-raising tale, and they're all true, too."

Merwin was glad, later that afternoon, that Peggy was occupied for a time in some work for Mrs. Tate, and that the doctor had gone off to fish, now that his mind was relieved about his daughter, for she wanted to be alone in her little expedition to the Coast Guard station. Old Captain Wareham, who was sitting on the veranda, greeted her cordially, if with a certain surprise in his manner, when she came up the steps.

"So you decided to pay us a visit at last," he said, fussing about to get her a chair and spreading a newspaper on it lest she smudge her pretty little white flannel frock. "We don't have lady visitors often," he apologized. "Never, I should rather say, an' the men don't mind what they sit on usually. Doc off fishin', I presume?"

"Yes, he's down the beach," answered Merwin, a little at a loss how to present her request. It seemed more courteous to visit a few minutes first with the captain, however, so she made no move to tackle the real object of her coming.

"Bad little accident you had the other day," he commented further. "Not a good idea, trampin' around the beach alone. Bad stuff. And quicksands ain't the only strange things you'll meet, either!" he finished darkly. Then he added: "Better take little Peggy with you after this. She knows where to go and where not. You feelin' all right now?"

"Yes, thank you," said Merwin. "I'm all right again; only I hate to think about the thing. It was too terrible!" And she shuddered involuntarily at the mere allusion.

"Yes, yes! We gotta distract your mind," the captain hurriedly responded. "Where's that Peggy girl today? You an' her ought to make a good team. She knows a lot, that little rascal; only she's a hard one to get acquainted with. Scared as a jackrabbit of strangers."

"Oh, we're splendid friends now!" exclaimed Merwin. "I think the world of her. But she's busy in the kitchen helping her grandmother.... I was wondering, Captain Wareham, if you'd let me go and look over those books where you keep the records of the wrecks and things. They seem awfully interesting to me, and as I haven't anything else to do this afternoon, I thought it would be a good time to look them over."

"Sure *and* certain!" replied the captain. "You jest go right into the office an' pull 'em down from the shelf—any you want. I kept 'em or superintended the keepin' of 'em these thirty-five years, and if you don't understand anything you want to know, jest ask me and I'll tell you the hull story. We ain't got room to put down much detail in them books. Here you are." And he led her into the little office where the books were kept.

CHAPTER VIII

The Number Three Surfman

A T FIRST THE old captain was inclined to linger about and explain the meaning of the different entries, and while he was present, Merwin took out volumes at random and opened them anywhere. But a sudden call from outside caused him to explain that he must be off on some business, and he apologized for having to leave her. It was with no regrets, however, that she saw him go, since when he was there, she did not feel at liberty to make the search she wished.

It took but a short time to find the volume labeled "1906" and scarcely more to turn to the date, "Jan. 29," where there was a more lengthy entry than usual in the old captain's precise, angular handwriting. Much of it was taken up with technical weather conditions from which she gathered the idea of an unusually heavy storm. Then, toward the end:

4.00 P.M. Four-masted schooner sighted off-shore about seven miles, under bare poles.

4.20 P.M.   Man on tower-watch reported same ship driving toward beach. Turned out crew and stood by on beach about ½ mile below stationhouse. Too much surf to launch surfboat.

5.30 P.M.   Quite dark. Schooner close to outer bar. Foremast and mainmast gone. Mizzenmast aslant. Flare burned on ship. Signaled answer from beach with Coston.

5.35 P.M.   Schooner passed outer bar. Pounding hard. Breeches buoy gear all ready waiting for ship to strike.

5.45 P.M.   Ship fast on middle bar. Mizzenmast gone. Gear set up on beach. Fired first shot line, but went wide to southward.

5.50 P.M.   Fired second shot line. Answered by another flare from ship.

6.05 P.M.   Hawser pulled out. #3 Surfman volunteered to board ship and was hauled out in buoy.

6.25 P.M.   #3 Surfman returned to beach with small baby found lashed to aftermast. Reported no one else on deck. Impossible to get below decks. Surfman bleeding about head from injury received while coming in.

6.35 P.M.   Hawser gear adrift and washing in. Sent #3 Surfman to stationhouse for medical treatment.

Note: Crew stood by on beach until morning. Plenty of wreckage came ashore, but no name found to identify ship. No bodies found. Baby, girl about six months old, not identified.

The account ended with another technical account of shifting winds and abatement of the storm.

It was with a very curious sensation that Merwin read

this record of a past calamity—one so closely associated with the affairs of her new friend and so fraught with mystery. Over and over she read the bald statements but could find no special enlightenment in them—nothing that helped in the least to solve the perplexing riddle of Peggy.

She turned to other entries of that period but discovered nothing at all in them to arouse interest. Only one rather curious statement, entered on the day after the storm, seemed in the least connected with her quest. It was to the effect that the "#3 Surfman" had been found dead on the beach late that afternoon. This did truly have the aspect of a rather singular connection, and she determined to ask the captain about it if she could get a chance to do so without arousing suspicion.

Presently Merwin closed the book, restored it to its shelf, and went out to sit on the porch and await the captain's return. It was over an hour before he came back and sat down.

"Well, young lady, found what you was huntin' for?" he inquired.

The very pertinent question made Merwin fairly jump, but she soon realized that this was only a form of expression with the captain and had no particular significance.

"It's very interesting reading, isn't it, Captain Wareham?" she replied. "But there are a good many things in the records that rather puzzle me. For instance, I wonder if you could tell me about the breeches buoy and how it's worked."

Was she mistaken or did the captain really turn on her a rather keen and speculative glance? She could not definitely tell, for it had been such a fleeting look. But at all events, he began to describe to her the workings of the breeches buoy, taking her inside the boat room where the buoy was kept to illustrate more graphically what he was saying.

Merwin gathered that first a slender coiled line is shot from a little cannon or mortar out to the ship, and that by means of this line, the men on the ship pull out successively heavier lines till the heavier hawser on which the breeches buoy proper is run is reached and made fast to the highest part of the ship above water. The shore end of the hawser is made fast to the sand anchor, which consists of two pieces of timber fastened at right angles one over the other and buried in the sand by the surfmen. The breeches buoy is then pulled by the surfmen out to the ship and back by means of one of the ropes already dragged out with the hawser.

"That's the way it works," Captain Wareham ended the description, while Merwin, thinking rapidly, tried to decide just how to frame her next question. But all she could manage to say was:

"It all sounds very dangerous to me, Captain Wareham. Don't any of the men get badly hurt sometimes while they're working with the breeches buoy?" The question was clumsily put, she knew, but in spite of that it seemed to have had just the effect she desired, for the old captain started off on the very track on which she had wished him to take.

"They sure do," he rambled on, leading the way out to the veranda again as he talked. "I remember a strange thing about that very business of the breeches buoy that happened here some years back; 'bout twelve or fifteen, I reckon. We'd had a bad spell of weather for a week or more, high tides an' a great patter of rain. It'd washed in behind the dunes an' made the sand mighty shifty an' uncertain. Then she finally settled down hard no'east; regular livin' gale. An' right in the middle of it, a schooner piled in on the middle bar. We couldn't launch the boat—it was bilin' in like a volcano—so we rigged up the breeches buoy. I missed the first shot. The second one I put plumb over her. And a flare from the ship showed it had reached. And then we didn't get no more signals from the ship!"

It was at this point that Merwin recognized something familiar about the account and leaned forward involuntarily, in breathless interest, to hear what was coming next. The captain puffed meditatively for a minute or two and then continued:

"Minutes was gettin' mighty precious when one of the men he says that he would go out to the buoy. I told him he might be courtin' hurt or even death because the surf was fair alive with wreckage, but he would do it. So we pulled him out. It was about twenty minutes afore we got him ashore again. He brought a little baby, about six months old, with him, the only livin' thing left in the wreck. He was bleedin' around the head an' face from the crack of a piece of timber that'd struck him while he was comin' in, but it didn't seem serious. The gear broke adrift just after that, an' I packed him back to the station house, an' old Dr. Trenway, who was down gunnin' for ducks, fixed him up from the medicine chest at the station, an' he went to bed apparently all right.

"Next mornin' he complained of a headache, but we didn't pay much attention to that. Along about ten o'clock I seen him go down the beach and didn't think no more about him till around supper time, when I noticed he was missin'. Me an' one of the other men started out to look for him an' about a half-hour later found him layin' dead down by that old figurehead. Old Dr. Trenway said he must have died from a hemorrhage in the brain, caused by the crack on the head he'd got the night before. So you can see the men do get hurt sometimes."

With an elation she was careful to conceal, Merwin realized that the old captain had hit on the very incident she had wanted explained; there could be no doubt of it. A number of questions that she wanted to ask concerning it rushed into her mind. But before she could get a chance to frame one of them, Captain Wareham was again called away, apologizing, as he left her, for this new interruption. So her chance for further investigation that day was over, as she realized that it was time to be getting back to the hotel.

She sought a chance at the earliest moment to confide to Peggy what she had just learned but got none before supper time. And later, when all gathered in the big lobby about the stove, there seemed no instant when she could have Peggy to herself. She determined, however, to slip into the girl's room before they went to bed and there communicate the facts gathered that afternoon. Strangely enough, it was round the stove that same evening that a chance remark of Mr. Dillon, one of the visiting fishermen, led up to another disclosure on the subject uppermost in her mind.

He had been reading the paper while the others talked and looked up suddenly to demand of the company assembled:

"Remember old Clinton Warner? He used to come down here to fish once in a while. Haven't heard of him in some time, but here's a notice in the paper that says he was found dead in his office yesterday; been there all night, since the day before, and nobody could think where he was. Says he seemed perfectly well when he started out to business that morning, nothing in the world the matter with him. Seems he'd had a fall in his home the day before; stumbled over something and cut his head slightly against a sharp corner of some piece of furniture, but that was all. Didn't think anything of it and went to business next morning. Strange, isn't it? What do you suppose happened to him?"

"No, there wasn't anything very strange about it," responded old Dr. Trenway. "Happens more frequently than you'd think. The fall did it—caused a cerebral hemorrhage, no doubt, which didn't become apparent at once. There was a somewhat similar case, I remember, right down here. Remember that big storm in nineteen hundred and six, Billy—the hurricane we had in January?"

Billy Tate, who was sitting with his feet up on a ledge of the stove, one free arm around Peggy, glanced uneasily at the old doctor, nodded, and answered:

"Yep, it *was* a big one, but it wasn't a patch on that buster we had in nineteen-thirteen. 'Member how that licked up here over the dunes, and we thought the hotel was a goner for sure?"

Merwin, sitting by her father, half listening, half buried in a book, had pricked up her ears at the doctor's question, so strangely allied with what was occupying her own thoughts, and she watched and listened intently for Billy's answer. It was perfectly evident to her, when it came, that Billy was anxious not to discuss the incident and was trying to turn the doctor's mind to another affair. But the old doctor was not to be side-tracked. He had a tale to tell, and he was going to tell it, Billy or no Billy.

"It wasn't so much the storm as what happened after that wreck we had that I'm going to tell about," he persisted. "Do you remember, Billy, the schooner that went to pieces on the middle bar and how one of the men from the Coast Guard went out in the breeches buoy? I was right there on the beach and saw him pulled off, and it didn't seem possible that any human being could live in that smother of timber and wreckage. But he did! Came back apparently all right, except that he was cut about the head a bit. I looked him over and patched him up, but it didn't seem serious. And yet he died the next afternoon after wandering about the beach all day. Same kind of thing exactly as that Clinton Warner case."

Merwin glanced at Peggy during this recital and found her listening, with strained, intent gaze fixed on the old doctor. But it was Billy's expression that was the most noticeable. It was plain that, if he could have bound and gagged the narrator, he would have done so gladly.

"Yep, it was a fine thing," he hastily interjected, glancing sideways at Peggy, "a fine thing."

It was obvious that Dr. Trenway was not yet through. "I was always somewhat curious about that surfman. I'd noticed him about the beach a good deal, and once in a while his actions seemed to me rather singular. He used to spend a lot of his off-time rambling round the beach, and I always had the impression he was hunting for something—I don't know why. He just had that air. And the day of the wreck, I saw him fully half a dozen times on the dune up there by the figurehead, sweeping the horizon with a pair of marine glasses. He wasn't young—must have been over sixty—and it always seemed to me rather remarkable that a man as old as he should volunteer to go off in the breeches buoy. The older surfmen usually leave that job to the younger fry. But he would go, though the captain tried to persuade him not to. . . . By the way, I wonder whatever became of the baby he brought to shore. It *was* a baby, wasn't it? I had the impression that it died in a few—"

There was a loud crash at this point, and everyone fairly jumped. But it was only Billy Tate, who had accidentally (so he laughingly explained) pushed over the coal scuttle with his foot and sent its contents scattering over the floor. In the scramble to collect and replace the coal, the doctor's narrative was temporarily forgotten, and before it could be resumed, Billy had sent Peggy off to bed. Dr. Scott also seized the moment to shoo Merwin away to her rest, and she shortly followed Peggy. And whether or not the recital was ever resumed, she never knew.

But, sorry as she had been for the anxious moments the recital had obviously caused Billy, she felt that two points were now established beyond doubt. She could no longer question the mysterious connection between the affair of that wrecked schooner of January 1906 and Peggy. And the curious account of the Number Three Surfman must, she felt, be also interwoven with the riddle in some inexplicable way.

The first surmise she hid deeply in her own thoughts. But the second she discussed and re-discussed with Peggy before they went to sleep that night.

"I'm going to try to find out something more about that man," she announced finally. "Don't they have a drill with the breeches buoy every so often up at the station, Peggy?"

"Yes, every week. Let's see . . . I think it's tomorrow they have it. But what's that got to do with all this?"

"I want to watch it," declared Merwin. "Perhaps it will give us some new ideas. I've only seen it once, anyway, the first morning after I came. I think it's fascinating to watch. Let's go tomorrow."

Peggy agreed, and the two girls separated for the night. But next morning, bright and early, they were racing up the beach in the direction of the station and were just in time to perch on the dunes and behold the men dragging out the cart and paraphernalia for the breeches buoy, to go through the weekly practice under the eye of Captain Wareham.

It was an old story to Peggy, but Merwin watched with breathless interest while they went through the rapid movements of the drill. She saw old Captain Wareham squint along the little brightly polished mortar. Shortly came a low boom that made her jump, and high through the air went the heavy slug with its slender line, straight as an arrow over the crossarm aimed for, on which stood young Jim McCleod, a broad grin on his good-natured face. Then followed in rapid succession the different steps necessary, and the drill was over. The entire thing took but a few minutes, Peggy told her, and if there was a delay, the old captain demanded—and in no gentle terms—the reason. When the men were replacing the gear, Merwin suddenly turned to Peggy and gripped her arm.

"I've got an idea," she whispered. "It just came to me while we were watching the drill, and I was trying to picture how it must have looked that day of the wreck. We've got to know the *name* of that man, the Number Three Man who went out in the breeches buoy. Why didn't we think of it before?"

Peggy nodded. "I *did* think of it," she confessed, "but afterward I didn't think it would do much good if we did. But how are you going to do it? Who knows the name, I'd like to know?"

"There's only one person likely to know it besides your grandfather—and I think we'd better not ask him—and that's Captain Wareham. I do believe I'll go and ask him right out this afternoon. You see, we were talking about it yesterday and were interrupted. It wouldn't be strange if I just happened to mention it again because I was interested, would it?"

Peggy seemed doubtful about this but finally agreed that it would do no harm to try, if it could be brought about in a way that was natural. And so, that afternoon, Merwin again trudged up to the station, electing to go alone as she suspected that in this way she could obtain better results. She found the captain and sat down to chat with him as if it were the most ordinary thing in the world for her to make a daily pilgrimage in this direction. She believed the old captain so considered it.

They talked long and uninterruptedly that afternoon about Coast Guard doings, and Merwin deliberately kept the conversation as far away as possible from the subject that was uppermost in her thoughts. Indeed, she encouraged the old captain, finally, to give long accounts of his boyhood and youth, which he had spent in the service. And it was not till just before she rose to go that she reverted to the topic of yesterday's conversation.

"I just don't seem able to forget that wonderful story you told me yesterday," she began nervously, striving to keep her voice steady. "I thought of it all night: that poor man being dragged in the breeches buoy through all that wreckage and dying afterward from the injury! He must have been a splendid, brave fellow. Did you know him very well, Captain?"

"No, I didn't know him ... exactly *well*. Nobody did. He

was always a sort of mystery around here. Come out of no one knew where and got me to take him on as one of the crew. He was kind of old for the job, but I was short a man at the time and he did his work well, so I signed him on. Never mixed much with the men nor talked much to me. He was here about a year, I reckon, before he died."

"What was his name?" inquired Merwin innocently, but with a swiftly beating heart.

"His name? ... Let's see." Captain Wareham scratched his grizzled head and concentrated for a couple of intense moments. "So many of 'em comes an' goes, it's hard for me to carry 'em all. Near's I can remember his name was ... um ... Thomas ... er ... er ... *Gilchrist!*" he ended triumphantly.

Merwin got away after that somehow—she never could quite remember how she took her leave of the captain—and rushed back to Peggy with the news of her success. But when Peggy heard it, she did not seem quite so much impressed as Merwin had confidently expected.

"Well, you certainly got the name," she commented, "but now I don't quite see what good it's going to do us after all."

"You *don't?*" cried Merwin, amazed. "Why, Peggy! I thought you'd see right away! Don't you realize what 'Thomas Gilchrist' stands for?"

But Peggy only shook her head.

"*The initials 'T.G.' of course!—in that letter!*"

"I ... I never thought of it!" stammered Peggy.

CHAPTER IX

What Old Dr. Trenway Remembered

IN THE WEEK that ensued after the last singular discovery, the two girls spent the greater part of their time at the foot of the old figurehead, going over and over the contents of the work box, examining every article with the most careful and thorough scrutiny. The little gold thimble Merwin polished and polished, discovering the initials "M. R. T." on the band. This was the only discovery resulting from their patient study. Again and again, they read over and discussed every sentence of the letter and the diary in the light of what new knowledge they had, but it led them nowhere except to the very obvious conclusion that "T.G." or Thomas Gilchrist, the Number Three Surfman of that time, had joined the Coast Guard for reasons connected with this letter and had perished in the attempt to rescue those on board the ill-fated schooner in whom he was interested.

They did not again allude to Peggy's own supposed

connection with this matter, though the thought was uppermost in the minds of both. But apart from their conferences together, Merwin had been doing a good deal of thinking and speculating, and as a result she had reached some strange conclusions. Though she dared not disclose the fact to Peggy, she was now firmly convinced that the bronze-haired girl was undoubtedly one with the baby who had been brought ashore that wild night in the breeches buoy. After what her father told her and the curious coincidence of the diary, there could not be the slightest doubt of that. If there had been any, they would have been entirely dispelled by Billy Tate's peculiar conduct on the night the old doctor had recalled the affair.

Granted, then, that Peggy and this child were one and the same, in view of the mystery that had come to light about this baby girl of fifteen years ago, was it right, Merwin debated, to keep the matter secret any longer? Should it not be told and some sort of investigation be set on foot? If Peggy would only consent to it, they could talk it over with her father, if with no one else for the present, and trust to the wisdom and judgment of Dr. Scott to guide them further. But this she felt it disloyal to do without Peggy's consent, and yet, to ask for it, she knew instinctively, was worse than useless just then.

Then she began to wonder if it would be possible for her to discuss some of its details with her father without his suspecting her of having any motive aside from idle curiosity or without violating in any way her promise to Peggy. But even this, without Peggy's consent, seemed to involve a sort of violation of the girl's implicit confidence in her, and she decided against it. Finally, one night just before she fell asleep, an idea occurred to her, and she determined to tell Peggy of it at the first opportunity.

The following morning dawned windy and wet, with a heavy northeast gale blowing and the rain descending in torrents. Most of the fishermen decided against pursuing sport in the face of such a storm and gathered about the stove in the lobby or plodded up to the Coast Guard station to chat with old Captain Wareham. Dr. Scott was busy disentangling his favorite fish line and rewinding a reel and had told Merwin he would need her help in a little while, when he would call her. In the interval, she put a question to Peggy while the two girls were alone in the kitchen drying the dishes for Grandma Tate.

"I've been thinking of something, Peggy," she began. "There is one thing in this mystery that we've never had any light on yet nor tried to find out anything about, and it seems pretty important to me. It's all that about 'Jonas Tow.' It strikes me he must have been known around here because it must have been here that he was or that Thomas Gilchrist wouldn't have been following him about all the time, as he said he had been in that letter. Have you ever heard anyone speak of him?"

"No, I never have," Peggy assured her.

"Well, do you think it would do any harm if we were to ask someone?—my father, or Mr. Tate, or—"

"No, no!" cried Peggy, upset at once by this suggestion. "I wouldn't ask anyone! Not for anything."

"But would you mind if I did?" persisted Merwin. "In some way that no one could connect with anything personal? I'd just casually ask my father, for instance, if he'd ever heard of a Jonas Tow living around here some years ago. And if he asked me how I had come to hear about him, I could say that I'd heard you mention the name. That would be strictly true, you know and yet wouldn't be telling him anything you wouldn't want known. If he'd heard of him, we might learn something interesting, and if he hadn't, why there wouldn't be any harm done. What do you think?"

But Peggy's impressions were not favorable, argue as Merwin might.

"What if he asks you all sorts of questions about how we came to be talking about . . . that man?" was her final objection.

"Oh, Peggy!" Merwin cried in despair. "Daddy isn't as suspicious as all that! What in the world would he care how we came to be talking about him or why we had any interest in him? He would merely tell me if he'd heard anything about the man. And if he hadn't, he'd say so and talk about something else. You mustn't think everyone suspects us of having a secret and a mystery; nine cases out of ten, they're not thinking anything about us."

"Well, I'll think it over a little, and then I'll try to decide," was all that Peggy would concede. And Merwin went off to help her father rewind his reel and disentangle his line, wondering impatiently how in the world she was ever going to bring Peggy to see reason. Yet, after all, it was Peggy herself who came to Merwin that afternoon with another proposition and—for her—a rather surprising one.

"I've been thinking of something," she began. "You know, it's old Dr. Trenway's last day here. He's leaving for New York tomorrow morning, and he says he can't tell whether he'll ever come back to the beach or not 'cause he's going out to live with his daughter in California soon, and he says he's too old to be traveling back and forth across the country. He thinks it's likely he'll *never* come back. Now, he knows an awful lot about the beach and old times here; more even than Grandpa Tate, because he came here before Grandpa was born. And I heard him say once that he'd studied up a lot about its history, too. I don't reckon I'd mind very much if we could get a chance to talk to him this afternoon. For he's going away tomorrow anyhow, and he'd probably forget all about it afterward; and I likely wouldn't ever see him again. What do you think?"

Merwin thought the idea a capital one and said so without hesitation, and they began to lay plans for waylaying the old doctor that afternoon when he was off somewhere by himself. It was agreed that Merwin should be the spokesman and that Peggy was to play no part whatever except that of listener. But the chief difficulty was to get a chance to talk to him when no one else was around. It being his last day—possibly the very last he would ever be there—he seemed to be a most popular person that afternoon and was constantly surrounded by his fellow guests. The old gentleman would have been more than a little astonished had he realized with what anxiety two girls were watching the situation from a far corner of the room and speculating on the possibility of ever having a chance to converse with him without onlookers or listeners.

"It's no use!" sighed Peggy, as the afternoon waned. "If only it had been a decent day, he would have likely gone out for a walk. But this storm has kept them all indoors, mostly, and tonight they'll all sit around the fire till late, and we'll get sent to bed—and that'll be the end of it."

But the weather was inclined to be kinder to them than they had dared to hope. The rain stopped, the wind whipped around to the northwest, and the clouds broke by half-past four; whereupon all made a beeline for outdoors. The girls heard Dr. Trenway declare that he was going for a last walk before his departure—his usual beaten track along the foot of the dunes on the ocean side north to a certain point on the beach where he always turned in, crossed the dunes, and returned by a path that led along the edge of the bay. Quickly they made their plans.

"Let's run along back of the dunes a way and come out to the beach side just a little ahead of him," suggested Peggy. "If he meets us that way, he'll likely stand and chat, and then we can just walk along with him. He always likes company, and I've often walked with him that way."

The scheme worked as they had intended it should; the old doctor unsuspectingly welcomed their company and invited them to go with him on his late-afternoon stroll. He would have been decidedly surprised had he realized with what joy they welcomed his invitation. And in many ways, the interview was destined to stand out in their minds for years after with startling distinctness. A crisp, biting northwest wind, salt-laden, a late golden sunset sky, the heavy boom of the breakers with spray flying back from their crests as they thundered in would always remind the two of that last walk with Dr. Trenway.

For a time they let him choose his own topics of conversation and had no need to say anything for themselves, as he was a famous monologist. With tale after tale did he regale them—of his exploits on the fishing beach and even some of his experiences as a colonel in the Civil War. Merwin had decided to make no attempt to stop him or interrupt till there seemed a favorable opportunity for the question she wished to put. It came at last, after he had finished telling them of a curious wreck on the beach many years before at a place farther south of Barnegat.

A French vessel bound from Havre to New York was lost off Beasley Point. She had carried a very valuable cargo, and after the storm the beach was strewn with silks, satins, rare china, and other rich merchandise. But saddest of all, a beautiful young girl was washed ashore, silk-clad and showing every evidence of wealth and luxury. She had been buried in the Golden Cemetery at that place, and her grave could still be found there.

The little couch of pathos in this recital caused the group to walk along in silence for two or three minutes, and then Merwin saw a favorable chance for her question.

"Have you ever heard of a Jonas Tow who used to live around here, Dr. Trenway?" she began hesitantly. "I think

WHAT OLD DR. TRENWAY REMEMBERED

I've heard people speak of him." She hoped her question did not appear too pointed and personal, and waited breathlessly for the reply. But the old doctor evidently considered it quite natural, for he responded easily:

"Old Jonas, ha? To be sure I have! I've seen him myself many a time. He's dead and gone now, but he had the reputation of being a great old beachcomber—regular shore-pirate, in fact. He had a hut somewhere behind the dunes about halfway between here and the Light, and it was filled with the weirdest collection of stuff he'd gathered from wrecks along the beach. There were some rather ugly stories going about concerning him at one time.

"I remember that when I was a boy and used to come here, there was a rumor of Jonas having found a treasure chest or some such thing on the beach or in some wreck that had come ashore. There was even the story that he'd killed someone who was supposed to be guarding it, but I reckon there wasn't much foundation for that.

"Anyhow, we boys (my cousin and I) spent days prowling around the region of Jonas's hut, trying to find out where he kept the loot, till finally he got exasperated and drove us off with threats we didn't dare to ignore. That was my only personal encounter with him, but I saw him occasionally in the years afterward, prowling about the beach, generally around dusk, poking and prodding in the sand with a big stick he used to carry and peering out to sea."

"How long ago did he die?" asked Merwin casually, at the same time squeezing Peggy's hand as a signal that this was a crucial question.

"Oh, about twelve or fifteen years ago, I should judge. I wasn't here at the time and only heard of it indirectly long afterward. He was said to have been found dead in his hut by one of the Coast Guards."

"Did they ever find his . . . his treasure?" was the next breathless question.

"Not a trace of it!" laughed Dr. Trenway. "To tell the truth, I doubt if there ever was such a thing. They ransacked his hut pretty thoroughly after his death but never found an article of any description worth looking at a second time—nothing but junk. Nobody ever bothered even to cart it away. There's one curious thing, though, that I remember in connection with Jonas. It happened when I was a boy. A barkentine came ashore here one night in a terrific storm—a regular West Indian hurricane, the kind they get here once in a great many years. She was blown right upon the shore close to the dunes, not far from Jonas's shack, and there she rested for the better part of a year, almost intact.

"But here's the singular part," the old gentleman went on. "There wasn't a soul on board her, not a single paper or log book or scrap of information to tell where she came from or where she was bound. She was a 'mystery ship,' all right. She seemed to have been loaded mainly in ballast, and there she sat, as big a mystery as that *Marie Celeste* you hear so much about nowadays. Even her name boards had been torn away. People thought from certain indications that she was a French vessel, but beyond that there was never a clue. The strangest thing of all was, however, that seven months from the time she was swept up on the shore, another storm almost as violent came along and swept her off again one night, and she was never heard of after. If you can beat that in fiction, I'd like to know it!"

"But what do you suppose became of her?" queried Merwin.

"Doubtless she went to the bottom that time due to the condition of her neglected hull. But we always thought Jonas knew more about that ship than he ever told, for it rested at a point very near his hut. But that's something we'll never know the truth about this side of eternity, I figure." The remainder of the walk back to the hotel was rather quiet. Dr. Trenway seemed to have temporarily talked himself out, or perhaps he wished to look about him and muse silently during this last walk he expected to take along Tate's Beach. At any rate, there was little or nothing said, though the two girls were full to bursting with the new ideas they had gleaned. But the spell of twilight was on them all. The honking of a flock of wild geese winging their southward flight over the bay was the only sound save the thunder of the surf, and Merwin would never after be able to dissociate the name of Jonas Tow with the mingled odors of salt spray and bay bushes.

In the waning twilight, they had almost reached the hotel when a figure, approaching them out of the half-gloom on the path they were traveling, passed them with a cheery, "Good evening, all!" and they recognized young Jim McCleod of the Coast Guard station. When he was well out of hearing, the old doctor once more broke the silence.

"Life's a strange thing!" he said musingly, halting at the foot of the hotel steps. "And that young fellow's case is a good sample of it. Speaking of old Jonas Tow, that young chap happens to be a great-grandson of his, though I doubt whether he knows it himself."

"He *is*?" gasped both girls. "Why, how strange!"

"No, not so very strange, after all," asserted Dr. Trenway. "I don't know anything about old Jonas's wife and children; they seem to have been all dead and gone before my time. But he did have one granddaughter, it was known, married to a Scotchman named McCleod. She'd always lived over at Toms River and would have nothing whatever to do with Jonas because he was such a disreputable old customer. But, strangely enough, Jonas took a great fancy to her little boy. Jim was a cute little fellow in those days, and she used to bring him over to the station when she came to see a relative of her husband's who was one of the men here at that time. But she wouldn't let Jonas come anywhere near the child. It was rather pitiful, too: the old man wanted to see the youngster that he used to come and peek in at the windows of the station when the child was there, but that's the nearest he ever got to him, so they said."

"But why was she so cruel as that?" Merwin exclaimed indignantly. "Surely it wouldn't have hurt to let the poor old man see his great-grandson once in a while. I think it was awful!"

WHAT OLD DR. TRENWAY REMEMBERED

"Well, you see, old Jonas had a bad name. Folks had told some pretty ugly stories about the things he'd done in the past. One of the worst was that he used to watch out when there was a bad storm and set false lights on the shore so ships would go wrong in their steering and get wrecked, and then he'd reap a harvest from his beach-combing next day. At any rate, Mrs. McCleod seems to have been terribly ashamed of his reputation and finally wouldn't even own she was related to him.

"And I believe it was said that young Jim was not supposed to know it, either. But it has always struck me as curious that Jonas should have spent his days wishing for wrecks to occur—if he didn't actually cause some of them—and now his great-grandson is devoting *his* life to trying to prevent them, or assist in saving the situation as much as possible, should they occur. Singular, isn't it!" And the old doctor turned and walked away up the steps.

"Was it worthwhile, Peggy?" demanded Merwin, when the two girls stood alone in the darkness.

"Oh, how can you ask!" gasped Peggy. "We've learned so much. But I don't know what to make of it, do you?"

"No, I don't," Merwin answered; "but I'm going to try to puzzle it out, somehow."

CHAPTER X

On the Trail of Jonas Tow

"THERE'S JUST ONE thing to do now, Peggy," declared Merwin next morning. She had scarcely slept the night before, so carefully had she been thinking over all they had learned from Dr. Trenway on that notable walk. Neither, it is safe to say, had Peggy had much sleep. They had met directly after breakfast for a consultation.

"I've thought of something, too," responded Peggy. "I wonder if it's the same thing."

"My idea is that we ought to find and explore old Jonas's hut if it's still standing. Do you think you know where it is, Peg?"

"Just exactly what I'd thought!" exclaimed Peggy. "Yes, I think I know where it is. It's a place about three miles down the beach toward the Light. There's an old shack that's all tumbling to pieces. It must be his, 'cause there isn't any other around. I was going to explore it once myself, but it's awful wild there, and something scared me . . . and I ran away." She stopped impressively.

"Something scared you?" queried Merwin, amazed. "Why, what in the world was it, Peg?"

"You'll laugh, I s'pose," replied Peggy shyly, "but it was something very strange. I was just pushing open the old door when there was a scratching and scrambling inside, and I was so frightened I turned and ran, and as I looked back I saw some big dark thing rush out of the door and into the bushes. It was all so quick that I just got a sort of glimpse of it. But I ran most of the way home, and I never went to that place again."

"But what could it have *been*?" insisted Merwin. "It couldn't have been a ghost; there aren't any such things. It must have been something real and alive."

"I've heard tell," whispered Peggy, "that there're wildcats around, 'way down there—immense big ones—and I believe it was one of them I saw."

"Why, that seems simply crazy to me!" laughed Merwin. "I've always heard that wildcats lived in the woods and among the mountains. I never heard of such a thing as their being on an ocean beach like this."

"They're not that kind of wildcats," explained Peggy. "Folks say they were once tame cats that had been on ships wrecked here long ago, and they got off in the bushes and gradually grew wilder and wilder, and now there's a regular breed of 'em, so wild that nobody ever gets near 'em or sees 'em close. But they're very large and very fierce. People call them the Barnegat cats."

"Well, of course that's possible," conceded Merwin. "But if that's the case, isn't it awfully dangerous to go poking around in that region?"

"I've heard that they aren't likely to attack anyone, but just run away 'cause they're so scared. Perhaps they would be dangerous if anyone attacked *them*, but I guess nobody's ever tried it. Let's take big sticks with us in case . . . anything should happen."

"I wish . . ." Merwin considered thoughtfully. "I wish we could have a whole day to go down there and stay, so we shouldn't have to hurry back just at the most interesting point, perhaps."

"We could ask Grandma to let us take a lunch," suggested Peggy, and at this happy thought they both rushed off to the kitchen where Mrs. Tate was making pies. She gave her consent, but with many directions and cautions about getting into danger. And they packed up sandwiches and apple turnovers with all the anticipation and delight usually experienced by explorers. Half an hour later, they were hurrying along the beach, walking close to the water where the sand was packed as hard as a floor.

It was a gorgeous morning after the storm of the day before. The crisp October air, an unbelievably blue sky and sea, the crunch of the hard sand under their feet filled them with an exhilaration the like of which Merwin had never experienced before. That, added to their zest for the expedition on which they were bound, made even Peggy quite forget for a time her possible tragic connection with the mystery and revel simply in the excitement of the present quest.

At a certain point on the beach about three miles from the hotel, Peggy designated that they had reached the place where they must scramble over the dunes and into the wilderness behind them. And sure enough, the first thing that met Merwin's eyes as they reached the summit was a dilapidated, tumble-down fisherman's shack, one side already fallen in—blown down, doubtless, by some high northwest wind from the bay.

"Let's eat our lunch right now, sitting up here," suggested Merwin. "I'm hungry, aren't you? And that'll give us more time to explore later." Peggy assented and, perched on the dune top, they devoured their sandwiches while they speculated as to just how many wildcats might be concealed in that abandoned and wrecked abode of the once notorious Jonas Tow. When at last they had finished, they descended the slope, armed each with a stout club of wood, and cautiously approached the sagging doorway. Suddenly Peggy stopped short and pulled Merwin back by the arm.

"Look . . . there!" she whispered, pointing to a spot in front of them on the sand. Merwin looked down and saw what appeared to be tracks, just a few of them, of some animal. They certainly had the shape of a cat's footprint, except that they were larger than that of any ordinary cat that Merwin had ever seen.

"Now will you believe me?" breathed Peggy. "They were made this morning."

"How do you know?" questioned Merwin, also in a whisper.

"Because the big storm last night would have wiped them out if they'd been made before. But see!—they're pointing away from the shack."

"What shall we do?" demanded Merwin. "Dare we go in with that . . . thing around?"

"I'm going to try!" decided Peggy courageously. "The beast's gone out—you can see that—and there aren't any tracks back yet. If there're any more in there, I'll come out in a hurry and we'll run as fast as we can. Let's make a big noise now—sing or shout—and if another's in there it'll probably come out. And stand away from the door while we do it."

The next act of the performance was so ludicrous that Merwin would have shrieked with laughter had not the consequences been so much in doubt. Peggy raised her voice in a wild "Ha-ha!" and she herself began to sing loudly the chorus of a popular song. Then they both fell silent, tensely listening for a response from within. There was none. Only the low boom of the surf answered their efforts at a racket.

"Is it all right, do you think?" breathed Merwin.

"Maybe we didn't make enough noise," suggested Peggy. "I'll creep over and push open the door while you do a little more shouting or singing. If nothing happens after that, I guess it's all right."

And so Merwin shouted at the top of her lungs: "Hello! Hello! Come out of there!" as Peggy pushed in the sagging door. But nothing came out. So, taking a firmer grip on their clubs, they timidly crept into the semi-darkness of the deserted shack.

When their eyes at length became accustomed to the gloom, it was to behold an astonishing spectacle. Never had either of them seen such an amazing conglomeration of articles as lay stacked on that floor and in every corner of the shanty. A casual glance revealed an old broken ship's binnacle, a battered medicine chest, empty, a piece of a companionway, tattered fishnets without number, a rusted and broken brass handrail, and a dilapidated wooden cradle. Sand had blown and drifted in over the whole accumulation, and there were many articles, half covered, that it was difficult to identify at all. The entire assortment showed unmistakable signs of past overhauling and examination.

"What a sight!" sighed Merwin. "How should we ever know where to begin to search through here?"

"It's all been searched through long ago," asserted Peggy. "I guess after Jonas died, the Coast Guards and fishermen didn't leave anything here that was worth taking. And if they thought he had anything like a treasure hidden here, they'd have mauled it all over right well. But I guess, from what the doctor told us, that he didn't have anything worth taking anyhow."

"Of course we can't expect to find anything *valuable* here, at least not in quite that way," declared Merwin. "But we *might* find some clue or trace of something that would be valuable to *us* because it would be leading us in the right direction. Let's begin to hunt now. I'll start over in this corner, and you can begin in that one. We ought to meet in the middle."

The search that ensued was both grimy and discouraging. Right through the pile of accumulated lumber and rubbish they worked, tugging and hauling as they pulled the various articles out and shoved them aside after examination. They met in the middle over a piece of broken ship's anchor, tired, discouraged, and unbelievably smudged with dirt and tar.

"It's no use!" sighed Peggy, trying to wipe off her hands on a piece of old sail cloth. "There's nothing here a bit interesting to us, and it's horribly dirty work." But Merwin was still undaunted.

"Wait!" she ordered. "Surely this isn't all there is in the place. Aren't there any cupboards or any other rooms that we haven't seen?" She peered around curiously and discovered the door into the lean-to, the part that had been partially blown down in some past storm.

"You can't get in there," warned Peggy. "The roof might fall in on us."

"Just the same, I'm going to try," answered Merwin, pushing it open as far as it would go and squeezing herself into the narrow opening. "Perhaps you'd better stay there, Peggy, in case anything happens and I need help."

The interior of this cubbyhole presented a rather different aspect from that of the main room. It had plainly been a bedroom. A dilapidated wooden bed stood half collapsed in one corner, the headboard broken in two where the roof had crushed down upon it. The straw mattress lay in the middle of the floor, its stuffing three-quarters out and scattered around—the obvious work of some earlier explorer who had hoped to find golden loot hidden in its depths. The only other articles of furniture in the little room were a broken wooden chair and an ancient bureau, every drawer of which stood gaping open.

Over to this Merwin tiptoed, peering into every crevice and gingerly turning over the few nondescript articles that remained in it. But there was nothing that promised the least interest concealed there, and she turned away, deeply disappointed, for there seemed no other prospect of success in this region, which she felt should have yielded them some rich reward. Before she returned to the other room, however, she felt impelled to examine the bed a little more closely. To this end she ducked her head and shoulders to avoid the fallen roof and scrambled across to where the headboard leaned, half bent over and partly broken with the weight of the timbers on it. Something about the partial view she had of the back of the headboard attracted her; she could hardly have explained why.

Suddenly, with a little half-suppressed cry of excitement, she called, "Peggy, come here, *quick*!" It took Peggy but a moment to reach her side, and her eyes opened as wide as her companion's when Merwin pointed to a strange, box-like excrescence on the back of the headboard.

"What do you suppose that's for, Peg?" Merwin

whispered. "I've never seen anything like that before on the back of a bed."

"There must be something in it!" exclaimed Peggy, now equally excited. "Maybe that's where Jonas kept some of his treasures. I don't believe anyone ever discovered it, because you see it was backed up close to the wall and probably didn't show at all. It's only since the roof fell in that you could see it, I guess. But we've got to be awful careful how we try to get it open, for if we move this headboard a bit, the whole roof'll fall in. It's all that holds it up."

Very gingerly they poked and pried at the affair, which on closer view proved to be an old cigar box fastened to the headboard with nothing but tacks. One narrow end, they found at last, was hinged and loose like a flap, and into this Peggy thrust her hand. But a disappointed expression crept into her eyes at once, and she exclaimed:

"There's nothing in it but a piece of paper that's sort of stuck in the bottom. Wait a minute and I'll get it out."

After some difficulty she drew it forth, explaining that it seemed very frail and she was afraid of tearing it. And when it had at last been extracted without damage, she laid it in Merwin's hands, and they went over to the one grimy little window to examine it together. It was a common piece of wrapping paper, folded lengthwise and across, greasy and thumb-marked and suggestive of much handling by none-too-clean hands.

Merwin unfolded it, and Peggy stood gazing at it over her shoulder. When it was smoothed out, both girls surveyed it with very puzzled eyes, and Peggy had just started to exclaim, "Now what do you suppose that can—" when Merwin suddenly grasped her arm in a tense grip and whispered, "*Listen*. Do you hear that?"

"What?" breathed Peggy. And then the girls clutched each other in a terrified clasp, for from the other room came a faint and unexplainable sound.

CHAPTER XI

A Clue at Last

FOR AN INSTANT sheer panic kept them both silent. The sound they had heard was a weird and uncanny one, a cross between a squeal and a snuffle, utterly unlike anything they could have named or the cause for which they could imagine. It came again, and louder now, and froze them anew with a terror that was all the more real because they knew they were pinned in and could not possibly escape without encountering the cause of it. Then, for another moment there was silence.

"Wha-what do you suppose it is?" gasped Merwin in a stuttering undertone.

"I . . . I don't know unless . . . it's that dreadful . . . wildcat!" answered Peggy, still clutching her companion. Then she suddenly remembered her promise to Dr. Scott to take care of Merwin, and she straightened up with a jerk. "But I'm going in to see!" she added courageously and loosed her hold on the other girl.

"Oh, no, no!" cried Merwin, trying to prevent her. "You ... you might get into ... something awful." But Peggy was determined: she shook herself free and squeezed out through the sagged doorway while Merwin peered after her, expecting every moment to see a terrible black form hurl itself at her friend.

But nothing untoward happened. The room, as far as Peggy could see, was empty of any menace, and she called back to Merwin that she could discover nothing wrong.

"But, anyhow, I think we'd better get right out of here," she added nervously. "I don't like the feeling of things, somehow. Bring that paper with you. There isn't anything more to find in there, and we can look at it out where it's safe."

Merwin refolded the paper and tucked it into her sweater pocket and followed Peggy through the narrow aperture. But while they were standing in the cluttered outer room, giving it one more curious survey before they left, again the strange sound assailed their ears, nearer this time and more easily located. Instead of rushing out, however, they stood their ground, and Peggy whispered to Merwin:

"I think I know just where it came from, and I'm going to see what it is."

"Oh, don't! Don't!" cried Merwin distractedly. "It might be the wildcat."

"No, it can't be. It came from under that heap of old canvas over in the corner," declared Peggy. She tiptoed across the room and deliberately raised a corner of a torn and mildewed sail. "Merwin, come here," she called softly after she had taken one peep. And Merwin also tiptoed across to behold five little kittens, evidently not more than six weeks old, squirming around in the nest where they lay.

"Oh, the *darlings!*" cried Merwin, putting her hand down to smooth their fluffy fur. But she drew it back in haste to survey a map of scratches delivered by the fluffy balls of fur, which had changed into snarling little furies at the touch of her hand.

"Come away!" laughed Peggy as Merwin ruefully surveyed the damage. "They're the wildcat's kittens, sure enough, and we'd not be any too safe if she should come back and find us here. She'd probably fly right at us if she found us here near her kittens."

They beat a hasty retreat and, leaving the dangerous vicinity, scrambled up to the top of the dune where they had left their apple turnovers for consumption when their expedition of discovery was over. And while they ate them, they took out and examined again the curious paper they had unearthed in the secret box back of old Jonas's headboard.

"What do you make of it?" demanded Peggy at last, after a long and silent survey of the contents by them both.

"Nothing . . . much," acknowledged Merwin. "It looks half like a map and half like a picture of some strange kind. And what's all this printing on it? It's awfully blurred, and the spelling is crazy. Wonder if Jonas did it."

They studied it again in silence. It was indeed a strange

A CLUE AT LAST

muddle. Rough and crudely executed on what had been, evidently, a bit of ordinary wrapping paper, what it might have been intended to convey could only be imagined.

"I'll tell you what I think," said Peggy at length. "This wavy line along the middle looks like the line of the dunes, doesn't it?" Merwin had to acknowledge that it did.

"And this thing at the left-hand end, colored dark below and light above, could be Barnegat Light, couldn't it?" Merwin admitted that, now Peggy had suggested it, she could see how it might be meant for the lighthouse, and supplemented:

"Then these wavy lines at the bottom perhaps are intended for the ocean?"

"Yes," agreed Peggy, "but what's this other tall thing at the right-hand end and this long flat, black thing near the middle, by the dunes?"

"Well, it's hard to tell, but let's try to read what's printed on it, and maybe that'll give us an idea."

There were three lines of the crude, half-illegible printing, all in capitals, combined with figures, and the whole looked thus:

LITE-N-6

HED-S-4

RECK-W-

"It doesn't seem to mean anything at all," mourned Peggy, surveying their find disconsolately.

"But it must mean *something*," decided Merwin, "or it wouldn't have been made in the first place. I kind of think that 'l-i-t-e' is meant for '*light*'; and that probably means

Barnegat. He has it here, on the paper, so that makes me all the more sure. But what can 'h-e-d' stand for?"

"Why, *'head,'* of course!" exclaimed Peggy. "You see, he could only spell things by sound, probably. And 'r-e-c-k' is *'wreck'*; that's easy. But what these other letters and figures stand for, I can't think. And what do you suppose he meant by *'head'?*"

"I know!—the figurehead!" cried Merwin. "There's nothing else around here that has anything to do with a head, is there? And besides, that must be what he meant by that other tall thing on the right of this old map—or whatever it is. But where's the wreck he mentions next?"

"There're plenty of 'em all along," answered Peggy. "The beach is strewn with 'em, on down from here, but who's to know which one he meant?"

"And what's the meaning of the single letters—and the figures? They must mean something, too." But Peggy had no answer to make to this and ended the discussion by saying that they ought to be getting back to the hotel if she was to be in time to help her grandmother with supper. Reluctantly, Merwin began to fold up the curious old paper in the creases in which it had originally been folded. But, as she did so, she glanced down at the outside and suddenly clutched Peggy's arm.

"Here's something we didn't see before. It's printed on the outside, awfully faint and blurred. I wonder if we can make it out?"

Together they bent over it and finally managed to decipher the single line:

FOR LITL JIM MCLEOD.

The revelation was so startling that for some moments they had no words in which to voice their thoughts. Instantly their minds leaped back to their talk with Dr. Trenway on the afternoon before and the curious statement he had made just at the last. Here, in some mysterious way, was a direct proof of its truth. There could be not the slightest doubt of it.

"What does it all mean?" presently demanded Peggy. "This must be for Jim; but what is it?" But a sudden light had dawned on Merwin.

"I know; or at least I *think* I do. Jonas meant this for a map, with directions about something. Perhaps he *did* have a treasure, after all, and he meant that his little great-grandson should find it. There *is* something pitiful about it all, isn't there?"

But Peggy was thinking along another line.

"Do you think we ought to tell Jim McCleod?" was all she replied.

CHAPTER XII

A New Factor

"WHY, PEG, I'M astonished!" cried Merwin, staring at her friend as they sat together on the edge of the dunes.

"Why?"

"That you should actually propose to let anyone else into your secret! It would be far more sensible to tell Father or Mr. Tate or someone like that and let them decide what's best to be done."

"You don't understand," answered Peggy quietly. "I wouldn't think of telling Jim the whole thing: only the part about our exploring old Jonas's shack today and finding this strange paper there that seemed to have something to do with him—Jim, I mean. If there should happen to be any treasure . . . or . . . or anything like that, don't you think he ought to know about it since the old man left it to him?"

"But have you forgotten," Merwin reminded her, "that if there was such a thing, it wasn't old Jonas's to give anyway?

For the letter you found in that sewing box said he had concealed it and that it rightfully belonged to someone else. So what right would Jim really have to it even if the old man did intend it for him?"

"That may all be true," Peggy stubbornly replied, "but somehow I feel as if it would be a good thing for Jim to know. If there *was* such a thing as a treasure, and we should happen to find it, I'd . . . I'd rather have him have it than . . . than keep it for my-myself. I'd . . . I'd never say a word about that . . . other thing I found under the figurehead."

And Merwin was keen enough to read the meaning underlying this rather curious statement. She understood that Peggy would be glad to settle the mystery in this way and let the question of her own connection with it rest forever untouched.

"There's another reason, too," went on Peggy, "why it would be a good thing to let Jim into this. He might be able to help us puzzle out old Jonas's map or directions or whatever they are and find the treasure—if there is one. I'm certain we'll never be able to do it ourselves."

But Merwin had one other objection: "You know Dr. Trenway said that Jim's mother never told him he was old Jonas's great-grandson. And I don't think it would be right for us to give that secret away now, since his mother never wanted him to know. What are you going to do about that?"

"We needn't tell him he was any relation to old Jonas," countered Peggy. "We can say we've heard that the old man used to be kind of fond of him when he was little (that's quite true, you know) and that he evidently left him something when he died. Wouldn't that be all right?"

Merwin had to concede that it would, and Peggy laid her plans to convey the secret to Jim next afternoon. Then they both decided that it was time to get back to the hotel.

A more astonished young person than Jim McCleod, on the following afternoon, it would have been difficult to find. He was just about to start out on his monthly twenty-four hours' leave and had come over to Billy Tate's to borrow the old man's launch to run across to Toms River in. As he knelt on the dock unfastening her painter, Peggy approached him and whispered mysteriously:

"Jim, don't go across yet—at least not for a while. I've ... I've something very important to tell you."

With rather ill-concealed impatience—for he had been counting on this holiday for at least two weeks past—he exclaimed:

"All right, Peg; fire away. Only be quick about it, or I'll be too late for the movies this afternoon."

"I can't hurry about it," declared Peggy and added with decided dignity: "It's something very important that concerns you, Jim. If you can spare about an hour, I'll explain it to you. If you can't, we'll let it go till some other time." And she turned away and walked back along the dock to the shore.

Jim stood up, shoved his hands into his pockets, and stared out across the bay. He was a slim, straight, dark-haired young fellow, light in build but with muscles tough and strong as whipcord. As a rule his attractive face was lit by a whimsical smile, but just at present it was clouded by a very glum expression. All morning he had been looking forward to that swift race across the ruffled blue waters of the bay. Half a dozen different attractions beckoned him from Toms River. And here was Peggy with some nonsense, doubtless, in her little brain, striving to detain him from his much anticipated diversions. He scowled at a swooping seagull.

No, it was too ridiculous! He'd simply tell her to keep it for the next afternoon. What could the child want of him, anyhow? He strode down the dock to inform her that her request was impossible to grant and had just opened his mouth to say so when natural curiosity got the better of him. After all, he *could* wait an hour or so and go to the movies that evening instead. Let the kid get her troubles off her chest. He'd listen to 'em, if it would be any satisfaction to her.

"Very well, Peg. I guess I can spare an hour or so," he heard himself announcing. "What's wrong? Get it out of your system."

"Come down along the beach a way," answered Peggy, "and Merwin and I'll explain it to you. I don't want to do it here."

Rather bored and yet curious, Jim followed the two girls over to the ocean and walked with them to the foot of the figurehead, where all three sat down.

"You tell it, Merwin," said Peggy. "You can explain it better than I can." So Merwin began by detailing to him a little of the talk they had had with old Dr. Trenway the afternoon before their recent adventure. This she gave as the reason they had decided to explore old Jonas's shack, just for the fun of the thing. Then she described to him their exploration of the hut and their find in the back of the old bedstead. Then, and not till then, did she display the curious paper, and Peggy pointed triumphantly to his name laboriously printed on the back.

"Now I hope you'll believe," she said, "that we had a good reason for saying there was something important that concerned you."

For a long time, Jim did not make any reply, but sat looking at the paper, his lips pursed in an inaudible whistle. When he did speak, what he said made the girls fairly jump.

"I suppose you know old Jonas was my great-grandfather," he remarked.

"Y-yes . . . we did," stammered Peggy, "b-but we didn't know you knew it. Dr. Trenway said your mother never told you."

"Oh, *sure* I knew it!" he declared cheerfully. "D'you suppose the fellers in school'd let a thing like that get by without informing yours truly? I heard that pretty near the first day I went to school. Mother was mad as a hatter when I told her what I'd heard, but I didn't care. The old boy was dead by that time, or I'd have got over to the beach and cultivated his acquaintance somehow. And so the old scout left me something, did he? Well, my goodness, we're going to find out what it is; and right now, too, if we can dope this out!"

He returned with such enthusiasm to the study of the wrapping paper that his engagements for the day were entirely forgotten, and the girls were both astonished and delighted.

"There's something in this, all right," he mused, mulling over Jonas's ill-spelled screed. "The poor old man never went to school in his life, I imagine, and probably all he knew about spelling and reading and numbers was what he'd picked up at odd times, just enough so's he could understand the value and meaning of some of the things he salvaged from the beach. Now, this thing is a map of the beach, all right, as you've guessed. And here's the Light and here's the figurehead. But what those other letters and the numbers stand for, I can't figure.... Wait a minute, though! ... Six and four? ... Six and four make ten, don't they?"

The girls assented to this very obvious truth. He stood up and stared from the top of the dune to where the distant shaft of the lighthouse showed faintly against the afternoon sky back to the great wooden figurehead above them.

"I should say it was about ten miles between the two, wouldn't you?" he questioned further. Again they nodded, wondering just where this reasoning was leading him.

"Then, don't you see," he suddenly exclaimed, "that what my old great-granddad probably meant was this: He was trying in his own way to indicate some spot on the beach that was somewhere between those two points. From it to the Light was six miles north; that must be what that 'N' stands for. And from it to the head it's about four miles south; that's 'S-4.' Get me?"

Now that he had worked the puzzle out, the girls were rather mortified to think that so simple an explanation had failed to occur to them. Why couldn't they have thought of that themselves?

"But what about the last line?" demanded Merwin. And Peggy answered her by exclaiming:

"There *is* an old wreck on the beach about four miles south of here. Don't you remember, Jim? It's the biggest one there left now, right close up to the dunes."

"Of course. And the 'W' after 'Reck' means *west*, then," he added. "Only, why Jonas didn't tell us how *far* west, like he did for the other directions, I can't see."

"It's very narrow there, anyway," suggested Peggy, "not half a mile wide, I should think. Perhaps he meant to go west straight in from the wreck and that would lead to it. But that's just in the worst of that awful tangle. Folks must have been right about thinking he hid something there."

"Tell you what!" cried Jim, suddenly all excitement, "we'll go and explore right now. You get your grandfather's big ax, Peggy, and those large shears he uses for cutting wire, and we'll dive into that dump if it's humanly possible."

"But you've got to go to Toms River to the movies," Merwin reminded him.

"Oh, stow that!" he inelegantly retorted. "What's the movies compared with a lark like this! Get those things, girls, and I'll go change into my old clothes. You better put something on you don't care about, too. You'll likely get torn to ribbons. Meet me down below here in half an hour; and please try to keep out of sight. I don't want the whole station following us up. The lookout'll probably see us, but he can't follow us for three hours."

Half an hour later, carrying a hatchet, a long-handled ax, and a pair of huge shears, the two girls crept along the dunes, keeping as much out of sight of the station lookout tower as possible, and joined Jim, who was crouching, impatient, in a clump of bay bushes.

"We'd better creep along behind the dunes for a little way and then get out on the beach and streak it," he suggested. "We've got three and a half miles to travel and no time to waste."

They passed old Jonas's shack on the way, and the girls were half tempted to go in and see if the wildcat was in the vicinity and if the kittens were as vicious as ever. But Jim urged them on, and the lure of hidden treasure was stronger than any other interest just then. It took an hour to reach the locality that Jim had decided was that indicated on the crude map, and there was the old wreck Peggy had mentioned, half buried in the sand.

Striking in across the dunes at this point, they came, directly they had descended on the west slope, to the most amazing and discouraging sight Merwin had ever gazed upon. As far south as she could see, and for a long distance north, the entire hollow back of the dunes was filled with such a wild, disordered mass of wreckage and old timber of every description, intertwined with a tangled growth of swamp cedar and bay and thorns that it baffled the imagination to see how anyone was ever to hew a path through it. Even Jim's cheerful face fell as he surveyed the appalling scene.

"The old boy picked a good place to hide the loot, all right!" he remarked ruefully, "I dunno how much impression we're going to make on all this, but we can only make a try at it. I'll take the ax, and you follow with the hatchet, Peg, and Merwin can bring up last with the shears. What we want to do is to keep going straight west, as I figure it. Here goes."

He plunged down the slope, the girls at his heels, and began to struggle with a tangled mass of "bread-and-butter" vine that was the first thing to block the way. This he clipped a passage through with the shears and then chopped down some bay bushes that grew behind them. He had expected to have to struggle and chop a way through innumerable pieces of timber and rotting logs, but, strangely enough, when the first two obstacles were removed, there came to light a curious, tunnel-like passage running right through the apparently impenetrable mass of ancient wreckage.

Someone plainly had been at pains to hew this out, far back in a former time, for there was every evidence, even now, that ax and saw had once been used on these helter-skelter odds and ends of logs and timber to make a way wide enough for a person to scramble through.

"My Aunt Maria!" exclaimed Jim, pausing to mop his forehead and survey the phenomenon. "It's the old boy's secret passage, all right. Come along. But hang on to your weapons; we may need 'em yet."

A NEW FACTOR

The girls were too awe-stricken at the singular revelation to reply and merely followed, breathless with expectation of what this quest was to end in. On and on Jim led, through the semi-twilight under logs and wild growths that intertwined them. Often he had to take the shears or the hatchet and open the way where it had been blocked by some recent growth. But at last he stopped short, merely remarking:

"This is the end, I guess!" He stooped down so that the girls could see, and they peered over his shoulder to behold a little rudely constructed shack with a door slung on two homemade leather hinges, now virtually rotted through, and only a wooden pin for a bolt. Jim extracted the pin after some difficulty, and the low door swung outward. A glance within revealed an old wooden trunk of some size standing directly and squarely in the center of the enclosure. Here, beyond all shadow of doubt, was old Jonas Tow's secret hiding place.

Jim bent and entered the shack, calling excitedly:

"Come on in, girls! We stand at last before the treasure chest." And as the trunk was obviously not locked, the hasp of the lock being sprung loose from its socket, he stooped and threw back the lid with a flourish, exclaiming gleefully:

"Here's where we lift the loot of the biggest pirate of the age!" And then his jaw dropped and an expression of almost comical dismay overspread his features.

The trunk was absolutely empty.

CHAPTER XIII

Dr. Scott Takes a Hand

MERWIN AND HER father were sitting on the screened veranda of the hotel one unseasonably hot and sultry afternoon, for so annoying had been the pest of flies and mosquitos that the protection of the screens was most welcome. The two of them had been quite alone, he answering a number of business letters, she absorbed in a book. Without her knowledge, Dr. Scott had been regarding his daughter for some time with a keen and speculative look. Presently he spoke:

"Is there anything that's bothering you, Merwin?"

She fairly jumped at the unexpectedness of the question.

"Why, no, Daddy!... That is... er... no, I don't think anything is *bothering* me exactly. What do you mean?"

"Well, I think something is," the doctor persisted gently, "if you'll just be candid with yourself—and me. I've been watching you pretty carefully, and you haven't seemed quite yourself for two or three days past. You are nervous and 'jumpy' and you haven't had so good an appetite as usual; you have the general air of brooding over something or other that's worrying you. Better tell your dad about it. You always have told him your troubles, you know. What's the matter? You haven't been having a scrap with little Peggy, have you?"

To his amazement, Merwin burst into a storm of sobs and got up and threw herself into his lap, burying her head on his shoulder. Without a word of comment, he let her sob it out, and when she had grown a bit calmer merely remarked:

"So it is Peggy, then. Can't you tell me what the trouble's about, honey?"

"Oh, we . . . we haven't had any trouble, any quarrel, or that sort of thing," hesitated Merwin, drying her eyes, "but . . . but we just don't agree about something. I . . . I wish I could tell you about it, but I can't. I've solemnly promised I wouldn't tell anyone. I . . . I've wanted to . . . to tell you all along, but she . . . she doesn't want me to."

Dr. Scott drew his brows together in a puzzled frown. That there was something more here than appeared on the surface, he was convinced; nor was it, he knew, merely some childish quarrel or misunderstanding. Merwin was too well balanced to be upset by any such trifle. No, it was something deeper than that, and while he did not care to force his daughter's confidence or cause her to break faith with Peggy, he felt it important that Merwin's cure should not be interfered with by any mental disturbance for which she could find no relief. Yet how to proceed in the matter was certainly a problem. He had never before encountered such a deadlock in his dealings with this beloved and only child.

While he was silently mulling it over and Merwin was recovering her poise, Peggy appeared in the doorway, plainly searching for her companion. Her presence furnished Dr. Scott with precisely the opportunity he was seeking.

"Peggy," he said quietly, "I want to have just a little talk with you. Won't you come and join us? Here, take this rocker. It's too hot and mosquito-y to be outside anyway."

Peggy came over in a hesitating way, for she sensed something unusual in the atmosphere, and took the chair he had indicated. Her big gray eyes turned from Merwin to the doctor in a questioning gaze, and she had the air of being on the point of fleeing at any moment. So Dr. Scott deemed it wise not to mince matters, but to come to the point at once.

"I want you to understand, Peg, before I say anything more, that what I'm going to tell you is strictly up to me. Merwin has never done or said the first thing to violate the trust you've placed in her, even to me. I just happened to discover a few little things for myself and feel that I ought to speak to you about them."

At this point, Peggy's startled gray eyes opened wider than ever, and she cast a questioning and somewhat reproachful glance at Merwin. But the doctor hurried on:

DR. SCOTT TAKES A HAND

"You know, my main concern down here is Merwin's health, and I've been watching her more closely than either of you has guessed, I imagine. For a while she was doing splendidly, but in the last few days I've noticed that she's nervous and excited and evidently rather upset about something, and it has worried me. I thought perhaps you and she had had some little misunderstanding, and I asked her about it today, and though she hasn't told me a thing, I figured it out that there is something that's bothering you both, but that *you* feel, Peggy, that you prefer the matter to be kept a secret. Is that true?"

Peggy nodded, almost against her will, feeling it impossible with those direct and searching eyes of his upon her to conceal the truth. She felt, besides, a wild longing to rush from the veranda and escape from his questioning; yet this, too, seemed quite impossible.

"Now, Peggy, child, please don't think for a moment that I want to pry into your affairs. I distinctly do not. I should never for one moment try to force your confidence if you do not care to give it. That isn't like me, you know. But I should like to say just this and have you think it over: If you should ever care to let me into your secret, you'll find I'll never take advantage of it or you in the slightest particular. Perhaps you may even be glad later that you have let me in. For I want to tell you something that may rather surprise you both. I think I have just an inkling of what that secret concerns, anyhow, though neither one of you would be able to guess how I found it out. So think it over, Peggy, and if you should decide to confide in me,

I know you won't regret it. If, however, you can't bring yourself to it, we'll forget all I've said. Only I must not have my little girl worry too much over something she can neither rectify nor tell me about."

He stopped there, and, in the dead silence that followed, Merwin held her breath while she watched Peggy, whose big gray eyes, the dark pupils now dilated to their utmost, were fixed on the doctor's face. What would her answer be?

When it came, it was different from what either expected.

"What is it that you know?" she gasped in a half-whisper. "How did you find it out?"

Dr. Scott smiled at her whimsically.

"You're trying to take an unfair advantage, Peg," he replied. "You want to know my secrets, and you won't tell me one of yours in return. Why not let's pool our interests and see what we can make of it all?"

It took Peggy a moment to construe this remark, but when its purport dawned on her, she drew in her breath with an air of decision. Afterward she confided to Merwin how it suddenly came over her that she was extremely foolish to keep it all to herself when she trusted Dr. Scott so absolutely. He was, after all, Merwin's father, and as Merwin knew everything and longed, herself, to confide in him, and since he evidently knew something about it anyhow, what was the use of keeping it from him any longer?

Suddenly all her barriers went down.

"All right!" she said. "I don't mind if you know. But Merwin must tell you. I can't. I don't want to be here when she does." And she turned and fled from the veranda, off and away over the dunes.

All through the long, hot afternoon, Merwin and her father sat there on the veranda while she recounted to him, meticulously, every detail of the mystery that Peggy had revealed to her and the progress they had made thus far toward its solution. She ended with the account of their expedition to old Jonas's hiding place with Jim two days before and its disappointing anticlimax.

"We were all awfully disgusted at it," she said. "Jim thinks that someone got in there at some time and stole it away and we'll never hear any more about it—if there ever *was* anything worth taking. And he's more than half inclined to think there wasn't, anyhow. He said it was good fun to go hunting it, and that old Jonas evidently did mean that paper for a key for finding the hiding place. But now he's lost all interest in it and says he's too busy to go hunting around any more.

"But of course he doesn't know anything about the rest of it," Merwin went on, "and Peggy and I feel that there's something awfully strange about it all. And what has made me so nervous lately is that I feel more and more that it isn't right for Peggy to keep this thing a secret any longer. I can't make her see that it might be very important for all this to be known—this thing that she has discovered. But she won't agree, or at least didn't till just now, after what you said."

Dr. Scott had listened to it all in silence but with an air of keen interest. When Merwin's account was finished, he sat for a moment with folded arms, gazing out over the dunes. Presently he spoke:

"I thought it was something to do with Peggy's origin that was troubling you, but I never dreamed that you'd stumbled on anything like this. Billy Tate has been worrying for some time past lest Peggy should somehow discover the fact that she is only his adopted granddaughter. He is almost foolishly nervous about it. He has wanted her never to know, if possible, but I have been trying to warn him that such a discovery will almost inevitably be made by her sooner or later. He has been in misery since old Dr. Trenway's unfortunate reminiscences the other night, thinking that Peggy might have begun to suspect something. He said he saw her looking at the doctor in the most startled way while he was talking and thinks she's acted differently ever since.

"Then old Captain Wareham—who by the way, also knows the secret about Peggy; the only one who does, besides Billy and Mrs. Tate and me—was telling me the other night that you had been examining some of the Coast Guard records recently and seemed more interested in the wreck when Peggy was brought in here than anything else. It made him wonder if Peggy had in some way stumbled to the fact that all was not as she had supposed about herself and had perhaps confided in you and got you to make some researches for her.

"And I," the doctor went on, "knowing that you already knew about Peggy, through what I had told you, and feeling certain that you would not divulge the secret to her when I had explained to you that Billy didn't wish her told, could understand the predicament you might be in and how the matter might be troubling you. But I confess I never dreamed how complicated and mysterious the whole affair is. There is something very strange in all this, and I think you two girls have done wonders in finding out as much as you have, especially when you were so handicapped.

"But now let's go and hunt up Peggy," he concluded. "I want to see the contents of the hiding place under the figurehead at once, but we won't investigate without Peggy's permission."

They went out over the dunes, Merwin once more restored to her usual lightheartedness now that she no longer bore the burden of responsibility she had been carrying but could shift it to the capable shoulders of her father.

"I do feel so sorry for Peggy," she confided to him. "It must be an awful thing to feel you don't really ... belong ... to the people you've always thought you did."

"Poor little Peg!" he answered. "Yes, it's a hard thing to swallow just at first, but not at all bad once you get used to it, especially if your adopted people love you as the Tates do Peggy. What's heartbreaking to me is the thought of her carrying her secret fear around with her all these years and never confiding it to a soul till she met you. That's real Spartan courage."

They found Peggy where they had rather expected she would be, sitting at the foot of the figurehead. Before they encountered her, Dr. Scott had already decided what his line of action would be in regard to letting her know what he knew of her history. He intended to take the same line Merwin had taken till after he could have a talk with Billy and warn him that it was useless to try to keep the secret any longer; that Peggy suspected and had far better be enlightened at once. Until then, he must appear to be as unconscious about her direct identification with the mystery as Merwin had pretended to be.

"Well, Peggy," he began, easing the tension in his usual direct and natural manner, "you two girls have certainly stumbled on a wonderful little bit of mystery! Merwin has given me a full account of it. Would it be asking too much to let me see the old box and its contents that you found buried under here?"

He purposely made no reference to Peggy's own connection with it and neither did she, but she began nervously digging at the back of the figurehead to unearth her secret. When she had made the hole big enough to pull the box through, she drew it out and handed it to him without a word. And they all sat silent, the girls watching him while he examined minutely its contents.

It took him a long time. The hot afternoon sun went down like a crimson ball, dropping into a huge black bank of cloud over the bay. The flies and mosquitos buzzed about the three in hordes, almost unnoticed, so absorbed were they in the fascinating riddle. Finally, Dr. Scott folded up the old letter, over which he had spent the longest time, and restored it and the other articles to the box.

"Would you care to trust this box to me, Peggy?" he asked. "I really don't think it's altogether safe down here on the beach, and you and Merwin would scarcely care to have it around among your belongings, I fancy. I'll keep it very safe and restore it to you whenever you wish."

Peggy nodded. "Yes, do keep it, please," she said.

"And I want to say something else," he went on. "I do deeply appreciate your taking me into this secret, Peggy, and I feel greatly honored by your trust in me. I promise you that I shall always respect that trust and never make a move or say a word to anyone outside about it without consulting you first. Is it your wish, Peggy, that we three work over this mystery together and try to see what we can make of it? If so, I'll go ahead with some investigations of my own, always with your sanction, of course."

Again Peggy nodded, a look of intense relief lighting her gray eyes, replacing the strained expression they had worn all afternoon. Then she and Dr. Scott and Merwin started for the hotel, the doctor with the precious bundle, well concealed in the old tarpaulin, under his arm. At the foot of the hotel steps, Peggy pulled Merwin aside and let the doctor go in by himself. And when he was out of sight and hearing, she clung to Merwin and half sobbed:

"Oh, I'm glad, glad, *glad* we told him! Whatever happens ... I feel as if I could breathe freer now. It ... it doesn't seem quite so bad."

"I knew you'd feel that way," was all Merwin could answer.

the great fire of driftwood on the blankets Mrs. Tate had brought down, poking at the apples that were sizzling in the embers, and holding marshmallows on pointed sticks over the blaze till they turned a crisp brown and their dripping, toothsome contents oozed out.

The doctor and Billy kept piling on more wood as the fire needed it and joking and poking fun at each other and Mrs. Tate and the girls, for all the world like a couple of boys just let out of school. Merwin decided that she had never in her life enjoyed an evening so much.

It was a very dark, moonless night, and outside of the ring of brightness created by the fire, scarcely an object could be seen in the velvet blackness. Only the crash of the surf close by told their close proximity to the water's edge. Presently two or three of the Coast Guard men rambled down the beach, attracted by the fire, and joined them. Among them was Jim McCleod. These promptly joined in the jollity, and presently they began to sing. One after another of the latest popular songs they sang in chorus till the repertoire of these seemed exhausted, and then they began on some of the good old standbys. Of this variety, Dr. Scott seemed to have an inexhaustible supply, and the concert finally developed into his singing the verses in his fine baritone and the others joining in the choruses. He had just rendered the last verse of "Loch Lomond," and they were all singing,

"For ye'll tak the high road an' I'll tak the low road,
"An' I'll be in Scotland afore ye!"

when Merwin turned to say to Peggy, "Oh, I *wish* he'd

brought his violin down here." Then she stopped and stared in utter astonishment. Peggy was not there, nor was she anywhere else in the circle about the fire.

For a moment Merwin thought that Peggy might only have run off up to the hotel for extra wraps, as she had complained of being chilly. But time passed, and Peggy did not come back. The men sang two more songs, and Merwin began to feel decidedly uneasy. Wherever Peggy had been, it was certainly time that she reappeared now. The doctor had just finished with a solo,

"*Drink to me only with thine eyes,*"
and Merwin had decided to ask Billy if he had seen Peggy anywhere when the girl herself slipped out of the darkness and into the ring of light and settled down again at Merwin's side.

"Where in the world have you been?" Merwin instantly demanded, but Peggy only laid a cold little hand over her own.

"Hush!" she whispered. "Don't ask me anything just now. I've something to tell you after we go up to the house."

From that moment Merwin could take no further interest in the doings about the fire, so devoured with curiosity was she to hear what Peggy had to tell. She was not sorry when, shortly after, the doctor announced that it was growing too cold for her to stay out any longer, and Billy, agreeing with him, began to cover the dying embers of the fire with sand. The station men started up one more rousing song before they departed—"Heave ho! My lads, the wind blows free"—and when it was over, tramped away up the beach still humming the chorus. And the jolly little beach party was over.

"Now tell me all about it!" demanded Merwin when she and Peggy had gone upstairs and were saying good night in the hall.

"Yes, I will," said Peggy, "but get your father to listen, too. I think he ought to hear it."

So Merwin called Dr. Scott upstairs, and in Merwin's room Peggy told her tale.

"I was watching when the station men came along," she began a little breathlessly. "I hadn't been looking at the fire quite so steadily as the rest of you, so I could see more in the dark outside it. When the men came up, there were only three of them, but I was certain I'd seen a fourth one sort of trailing on behind when they were farther away. I waited a while and didn't say anything 'cause I thought the fourth one would probably come along a little later. But nobody came. Then I began to get uneasy, wondering where he'd gone and what he could be doing, and I kept thinking of those footprints around the figurehead.

"So at last, when no one was noticing, I just slipped away and ran back behind the dunes and crept along in the dark as softly as I could, down to the figurehead. I kept back near the bushes all the time, so's to be hidden by them, but my feet would crunch some in the sand; I couldn't help that noise. I got quite close at last—almost up to the little shack—and suddenly I saw someone dash down on the other side of the dune and off into the bushes on the bay side. He must have heard my footsteps crunching in the sand and got scared and run off. I waited and waited there in the bushes, thinking perhaps he'd come back. But he never did, and I didn't like to be away from the fire any longer, so I came back. But there sure is somebody meddling around that figurehead."

"Did you catch a glimpse of him so that you could recognize him?" demanded the doctor eagerly.

"No, I was too far away. He was just like a big, dark shadow, and he got out of sight awful fast."

"Well, there's certainly something strange in this," decided the doctor. "I suppose whoever it was thought we'd be too occupied with the fire to notice what might be going on around the figurehead. But you certainly have your eyes about you, Peg! You were one too many for him this time. Now, you girls go to bed and forget all about it. I'm going to get on some warm things and spend the night fishing. And if I don't do some reconnoitering around that figurehead, it won't be my fault. Good night, both of you."

And he went off to prepare for his vigil.

CHAPTER XVII

Crab Meat and Consequences

WHEN THE DOCTOR appeared the next morning before breakfast, the girls eagerly demanded of him whether or not he had made any discoveries during the night.

"Not a thing," he replied. "I hung around in the bushes near the figurehead for two or three hours without the slightest results and finally went off to fish. But I went back several times and examined the ground pretty thoroughly. Whoever had been there earlier in the evening had probably been scared off for the night and didn't dare to attempt it again. We'll have to keep watch and catch him some other time. I came back at five and slept till now. After breakfast we might go over to the place and do a little more excavating. I'll get the big spade this time."

The girls agreed joyfully and were ready for departure soon after the meal when Mrs. Tate called them back.

"What do you mean, Peggy, child," she demanded, "by

CRAB MEAT AND CONSEQUENCES

going off and leaving all them there crabs to be picked out! I cooked 'em all last night and there they lay; going to spoil unless you get 'em fixed as you promised."

With guilty consciences, the girls turned back.

"I *had* forgotten all about them. You go on, Merwin, and I'll stay and get 'em fixed up. Grandma'll be awful mad if I don't do as I promised."

"Indeed, I'm not going on!" declared Merwin indignantly. "I promised as well as you. I'm not going to leave you in the lurch. Tell you what: let's take them and go and sit on the dock while we pick them out, and I'll try to get Daddy to give up the figurehead business for a while and come and sit there with us and talk over what he's been thinking out. He promised to do that last night and didn't get a chance."

The doctor, hearing of their predicament, not only agreed to come and talk to them but insisted he was going to help with the messy and somewhat tedious job of picking out the crab meat, and the three repaired to the dock out in the bay with a huge dishpan full of bright red boiled crabs. The weather being unusually mild and summer-like for October, they sat there happily in the sun, their feet dangling over the edge of the dock, and proceeded to reduce to empty shells and meat the great pile of crabs in the pan.

"If Mrs. Tate doesn't give us all the deviled crabs we can eat tonight, after this, I'll never pick another crab!" grinned Dr. Scott, digging out the contents of a huge red claw.

"Oh, never mind that! Please begin at once and tell us all you've thought out about the mystery," demanded

Merwin impatiently. And the doctor, smiling at her eagerness, began:

"We've got all the elements of a very pretty little puzzle here, but I'm blessed if I know how to fit most of them together. Take that letter, for instance, the one from 'T.G.' that was in the work box. From all we know, there isn't a shadow of doubt that it was written by that Thomas Gilchrist, the Coast Guard man who lost his life after the rescue of the baby from the wreck on January twenty-ninth, nineteen hundred and six. Probably you wondered how it ever came, box and all, to be in such a strange place as you found it. I did also but have figured it out this way:

"As we could see from the last entry in that diary, the one who wrote it evidently realized that there was a pretty serious situation arising due to that hurricane. Later she probably realized further that it was a life-and-death matter, as the ship was becoming dismantled and had gone aground on the bar. Her first thought would naturally have been for her child—how it might be saved, even if she herself were not—and also how it might be identified. In the hurry and confusion, perhaps all she could think of were the letter and the diary; maybe there was nothing else handy *to* identify it, and in such a crisis, she wouldn't have a chance to write anything herself.

"But," Dr. Scott went on, "were she to fasten these to the child unprotected, they would certainly be torn off and washed away by the sea in three minutes. The only available thing, no doubt, was this compact little wooden work box in which she could enclose them, wrapping the whole in some protecting material—the tarpaulin—and fastening the bundle securely to the child. As the baby is reported to have been found tied high up on the aftermast, we can only conjecture that she may have begged some sailor to fasten it to the highest point of safety, or he may have done it after she herself had been washed overboard or drowned in her cabin. There is probably no way in which this point will ever be entirely cleared up, but this is a sufficiently good guess.

"Well, when this Thomas Gilchrist came aboard in the breeches buoy, all he found alive on board was the baby on the mast, and he brought it ashore. If, as we suspect, he was the 'T.G.' of the letter, there must have been little doubt in his mind that this was the child about whom he had had the correspondence, and no doubt he discovered immediately the bulky bundle fastened to it which he must have appropriated and hidden about himself before he left the ship as there was no mention of any such thing in connection with the baby in the reports. In fact, it was expressly stated, 'no identification.'

"Some time that night or the next day, he must have hidden the bundle under the figurehead. I rather think it must have been next day, as it was right there he was found dead in the evening by the captain. Why he hid it there, we can't tell. Doubtless for temporary safety. I imagine he had no idea that he himself was so near his end, or he might have confided in someone so that the baby might be properly identified and cared for. His particular physical trouble is often unaccompanied by any realization, on the part of the person himself, that he is in a serious condition. He simply wanted to keep temporarily secret the baby's identity till he was himself able to cope with the situation. So much for that.

"Then comes the problem of hitching up this matter with the affairs of old Jonas Tow. We can't doubt the connection since that also is mentioned in the letter. Jonas Tow had something that evidently belonged to these people—to the mother and child, anyway. 'T.G.' calls it the 'J.B. treasure,' and what that can mean is certainly a puzzle. Whatever it was, old Jonas had always known where it was, the letter says. That would indicate to me the fact that this treasure wasn't something that had recently come into Old Jonas's hands but had been in his possession for a good many years, perhaps. Which is the one reason why it might be possible to connect it with the mystery ship of so many years ago, the one cast ashore near Jonas's hut.

"Now comes the matter of that little old book found in that ship by Captain Wareham when he was a boy—and what was written in it." The doctor picked up a huge red crab claw and regarded it speculatively before breaking it open with his knife. And the girls, their works temporarily suspended, waited in breathless suspense for his next remarks.

"The ideas suggested by that writing," the doctor went on, cracking the claw with his long, deft fingers, "are rather fascinating to me because they involve so much.

There's the name of Prince Murat, for instance. Do you girls know anything about him?"

Both shook their heads.

"Well, you wouldn't be likely to," he went on, "unless you'd gone a little more into local history. Prince Charles Lucien Murat was a nephew of the great Napoleon Bonaparte—Napoleon's sister's son. He was also, of course, a nephew of Napoleon's brother Joseph Bonaparte, one-time king of Spain, who lived for many years of political exile in Bordentown, New Jersey."

"Good gracious!" sighed Merwin. "I never realized we had any kings living around here in New Jersey!"

"Kings and princes, too," laughed the doctor, "for Prince Murat also lived there. And not only that, but they came over here to this very coast, right around Barnegat, to hunt and fish. Prince Murat was a famous hunter, and this region was his favorite stamping ground. There used to be an old hotel near Barnegat Light—it's been gone many years now—which was the favorite stopping place of the prince with his horses and dogs and guns. They say he was a man of immense height, and he used to tramp around all day through the marshes in a pair of enormous boots, tiring everybody else out but never getting weary himself. Can you see why I think it wouldn't be so very strange if he had something to do with this affair?"

The idea was so new to the two girls that neither of them could quite grasp its full significance at first. While they were struggling for words, the doctor went on:

"Perhaps, too, that would explain the significance of the

expression 'the J.B. treasure.' Why couldn't 'J.B.' stand for 'Joseph Bonaparte'?"

At this astonishing deduction, the girls fairly gasped aloud.

"Why? ... How? ..." they stuttered, unable to fit this conjecture into any of their previous surmises.

"After all, it wouldn't be so very surprising," Dr. Scott declared, shying a crab shell at an inquisitive seagull. "Joseph Bonaparte had his home there in Bordentown crammed full of valuables from every country in Europe, and he had more, hidden over in Europe in various places, that he hadn't had a chance to bring over with him. Would it be so strange if this treasure had been something that was being brought over for him, which had fallen into the hands of Jonas Tow in some such way as we have conjectured?"

The girls had to admit that it wouldn't.

"But there's the question of dates; that's confusing," continued the doctor. "The captain told me that that mystery ship was wrecked here in the year eighteen-fifty-nine. Now, I'm not accurate on other dates, but I'm absolutely certain that Joseph Bonaparte had gone back to Europe and was dead and buried long before that time. Of course, there's Prince Murat left, who died some time in the seventies, I believe, and he may have had something to do with it, especially as that old book has his name on it. He had lost all his fortune and was in rather straitened circumstances, I think I've heard, and his wife and daughters had to keep a select young ladies' school in Bordentown to eke out a living. So perhaps he was having some obliging friend in Europe send him over some of his uncle's long-hidden treasures to help out. Who can tell?"

"What a strange life . . . for a prince!" mused Merwin, lost in the interest of this new feature and forgetting for a moment their own problem. But Peggy was working along a different line of thought.

"Then . . . what about *me*?" she demanded suddenly, dropping her knife and turning to look straight into Dr. Scott's eyes. And he realized instantly where her quick mind had been leading her.

"I see what you mean, Peg," the doctor answered quietly. "Taking it for granted you were that baby—and you undoubtedly were—you want to know what bearing this all has on you." She nodded emphatically. "Well, I have to confess that I'm rather stumped there. The letter from 'T.G.' has one curious statement ending it, if you remember. He says something like this: 'God willing, the time has come when you may rightfully come into your own.' Now, that was written to someone who we think was, without a doubt, your mother, Peggy. If this 'J.B. treasure' was rightfully hers (and yours too), then she must have been some relative or descendant of those people, the Bonapartes or the Murats. I can't make anything else out of it, can you?"

This conjecture seemed a terrible shock to Peggy. Her big gray eyes dilated, and she got to her feet, shaking visibly with the intensity of her feeling.

"I won't be! *I won't!*" she cried, stamping her foot. "I don't belong to kings and princes. I'm Grandpa Tate's. I won't be anyone else's!" She ran from them up the dock and across the sands to the hotel and disappeared within it, leaving Merwin and the doctor bewildered by her sudden passionate outburst.

"Poor little Peggy!" commented the doctor in real pity. "I'm afraid all this is rather hard on her. She is so afraid that something may happen which will take her from this beloved spot and the people she has always considered her own. After all, the whole thing is only surmise. I wish I could make her understand that, in any case, she has very little cause to worry. Go to her in a little while, Merwin, and try to smooth things out. Here, these crabs are all finished now. Let's carry them up to the house."

Just at that moment, Jim McCleod strolled up, whistling, and stopped to exchange the greetings of the morning and to make envious remarks concerning the pile of crab meat they had accumulated. He did not linger very long, but before he left, he called back over his shoulder:

"Wonder what's got big Olaf Hansen? Been watchin' him for the last twenty minutes, digging like mad at the back of the old figurehead. He didn't see me or think anyone was around, I reckon. We were all supposed to be busy up at the station but him, and he begged off this morning 'cause he said he had a cold an' was coming up to see the doctor. I'll say he must have a bad cold if that's the prescription you gave him!" And Jim departed, chuckling.

CHAPTER XVIII

Peggy Makes a New Concession

THERE ARE TIMES when events follow one another so rapidly that before we have time to sort out and think about our impressions of one set, another has crowded them out of our minds. So Merwin found it that morning. She had scarcely grasped the idea of the new element the doctor had suggested in the mystery when Peggy's outburst diverted her thoughts from it. And before she could go to comfort her distracted little friend, Jim had exploded another bomb.

"You take this stuff back to the hotel," the doctor exclaimed to his daughter, "and I'll go right over and see what that Olaf is up to. We've got the intruder at last, I reckon!" And he piled the dish of crab meat and the knives into Merwin's hands and was off down the dunes before she could even answer. She hurried to the kitchen with her burden and ran out of the house and down the beach, anxious not to lose a moment of this exciting development. But when she was halfway to the figurehead, she met the doctor coming back, a disgusted expression on his face.

"I was too late!" he said ruefully. "The fellow had accidentally taken the alarm and decamped. Either he saw Jim prowling around or had been watching us and saw that we were no longer occupied on the dock. But he'd been there, all right. Digging away with something or other, for the sand's all thrown around. But he didn't make much progress, I figure. Probably he had to give so much time to watching us, to see that we were still engaged here, that it cut him short in the work. No doubt he thought he'd have a free field this morning with the other surfmen all busy at the station and with us so occupied down on the dock where he could watch us conveniently. He must even have known that Billy had gone over to Toms River for the day. Pretty neat little piece of calculation, I call it! It's a good thing you girls decided to pick over the crabs this morning; otherwise we mightn't have known who is the marauder who's trying to beat us to it in the treasure hunt."

"But how do you suppose he came to know there was ... any—anything to hunt for?" stammered Merwin. "I can't understand that."

"That we can't tell definitely, but there's one way in which he might have got wind of something that you probably haven't thought of. Do you realize that anyone in the lookout tower of the station can easily see a mile or more up and down the beach, and with marine glasses even farther? It's possible that Olaf may have been on lookout duty at some time recently and have seen you and Peggy, or perhaps all three of us, mysteriously digging and poking around that place. If he saw it more than once, it may very well have excited his curiosity. It *is* rather an unusual proceeding, when you come to think of it."

"Olaf is not a pleasant nor a particularly trustworthy character," the doctor went on. "He's the most recent comer; he has been here only a few months, and the captain does not like him. He tells me the man's shifty and unreliable, and none of the other men cotton to him much. No one there except Olaf would have concerned himself for a minute with this affair, even if he'd seen us digging every day."

"But what are we going to do about it?" was Merwin's next question.

"There's only one thing to be done," declared the doctor decisively, "and I'm going to do that at once. There's no use going to the station and accusing Olaf. He has as much right to be poking around the figurehead as we have, when it comes to that. And he'd probably deny everything anyhow. I'm pretty firmly convinced that what we want to get at is buried under the platform. That Thomas Gilchrist undoubtedly removed the treasure from old Jonas's hiding place to some more convenient spot where he could easily get it and get away with it without going so far. And where else could he conceal it more successfully and easily than right there? He evidently thought it a safe enough hiding place for the other thing, so I take it that he no doubt used it for the treasure, too.

"I propose to take the afternoon and dig there until I have some reason to think we've exhausted the possibilities of the place. It's a very good time to do it with Billy away for the day and not around to ask questions. Meantime, you go up and see what you can do toward comforting Peggy. Explain all that has happened since she ran off and what I'm planning for the afternoon. And for goodness' sake, try to make her understand that even if she's descended from the Queen of Sheba, there's little likelihood that anybody will use that fact to get her away from Billy and Mrs. Tate!"

The doctor and Merwin grinned understandingly at each other, and she hurried off to the task of consoling Peggy. At dinner, she reported that Peggy had been very obstinate about it all at first, panic-stricken lest the new developments should mean changes and unhappiness for her. But after a while Merwin had been able to convince her that nothing untoward threatened; that the doctor and her grandfather would see that no harm came to her, and that she must join the new exploring expedition.

The doctor made his plans for the afternoon along more scientific lines than their previous attempts had been. Armed with planks and a spade, the three trudged away to the figurehead directly after dinner, Merwin having for once successfully begged off from her daily nap. Without loss of time, the doctor began the digging, starting as close as possible to the board of the platform and shoring up the sides of the tunnel he was excavating with the planks they had dragged to the spot. In this way the fine sand was kept from pouring back into the hole as he dug, and progress was decidedly more rapid. The two girls kept a watch in every direction in order to report the approach of intruders, and the doctor worked on with untiring energy. All became visibly more excited as the tunnel grew deeper and the space where the boarding had been cut away came to light.

"Here, Peggy," said the doctor at length, almost breathless from the speed with which he had been working, "take this electric torch and see if you can get down in there far enough to stick your head into that opening and look around in it and tell us what you see. You're the smallest and the one who can most conveniently get into the trench. I'm much too big for it as it is at present."

Peggy obediently turned on the torch, scrambled down into the narrow trench, and thrust the light inside the opening. Then, lying flat, she could just manage to get her face in at the hole through which she had once been wont to thrust her hand and arm and draw out the box. For a long time she lay thus, gazing into the depths under the figurehead, and above her the other two waited in keen suspense. At last she drew her head out and scrambled up.

"I don't see a thing ... that's interesting," she announced to her disappointed audience. "There seems to be just sand there, nothing but sand, and the boards at the sides of the platform."

"Oh, me!" sighed Merwin, disgustedly. "I was sure you'd

see a treasure chest standing right there, ready for us to haul it out!"

"Well, *I* didn't," grunted the doctor, rubbing his blistered hands. "That would be a bit too easy. But I thought perhaps there might be some sign of digging or a condition in the sand that would show the location of the thing. At any rate, we've learned *some*-thing. Olaf didn't get in here to pry around, or we'd have found traces of it. Now we'll just have to peg away and dig a wider and deeper opening and then crawl in somehow and dig *under* the platform. That's undoubtedly where the loot is hidden this time."

After a little breathing spell, he went at it again, and Peggy and Merwin were sent along the beach to hunt up more planks with which to shore up his tunnel still further. After an hour and a half of continuous work, the tunnel had grown two feet deeper and considerably wider, and the explorers were rewarded by finding that here the boards had been sawed away from the foundation of the platform to a sufficient width to allow an adult figure to pass through, with some squeezing.

At this point the doctor sat down to get his breath and ease his blistered hands.

"Give me a few minutes to rest," he panted, "and then we'll sail in and finish up the job. Though how I'm going to do much digging in that confined space is something of a poser. However, if it was done once, it can be done again. Meantime, you two can go in very carefully—don't knock down those planks—and just poke around and tell me how the land lies."

Merwin and Peggy immediately acted upon his suggestion but came out before long to report that there was nothing within to indicate that anything had ever been buried there; nothing but a fairly level floor of sand with the boards of the platform above and around the sides.

"All right, then," Dr. Scott replied, getting up to continue his work, "now that I've had a rest, I feel more like finishing it up. Guess my best move will be to begin in the middle and work out to the sides. One of you will have to stay in the opening and hold the torch so that I can see what I'm doing."

Again the tiresome work of digging began, this time under decidedly more hampering conditions. A deep hole in the center revealed nothing. Then the doctor had to fill that one in and begin on one of the corners. When he had dug to the depth of two feet or more in the fourth corner without the slightest result, he squeezed himself out of the opening and threw down the spade with an expression of disgust.

"It's no use!" he exclaimed in deep disappointment. "Nothing *could* have been buried in there any deeper than I've dug; it isn't humanly possible, considering the confined space. And I've gone over every foot of the ground. Either the treasure never *was* buried in there, or it was dug up long ago, which isn't at all probable, considering the fact that the other things were still in here. I'm fully convinced that it's somewhere else, after all. Let's fill this tunnel in now—it won't take long—and call it a day. I confess I'm tired out."

The girls joined in the work of pushing the sand back into the tunnel, leaving the planks as they were, and presently the spot looked just about as it usually did. Then they trudged wearily back to the hotel, feeling decidedly depressed and disappointed by the day's work.

"Never mind," the doctor said consolingly as they sat around the lobby stove (for the night had turned chilly), waiting for supper. "We've gained several things today, though the outcome did seem disappointing. We know who it is that's trying to get in on our secret. And we know further that it won't do a bit of harm now for him to dig away under the figurehead. Let him dig to his heart's content; he won't find anything there! And we know, beyond that, that our own search has got to be in some different direction. I'll think it all over tonight, and we'll begin on a new trail tomorrow."

Needless to say, the two girls were immensely cheered by his infectious optimism and his determination to continue along other avenues. After all, the day had *not* been wasted, for several questions had been settled and several more new lines of conjecture opened up.

"But there's one thing I do want to beg," he continued gravely, "and Peggy must be the one to grant me this permission. I want her to let me confide this entire story to old Captain Wareham. I have several excellent reasons for this," he continued, noticing Peggy's startled and reproachful look. "The most important is that I think he can tell me a number of things I want to know about that one-time Number Three Surfman, Thomas Gilchrist. But

I can't ask the questions I want to ask unless I can tell the whole story.

"And he can also help me keep an eye on Olaf and see that he doesn't butt in on any more of our investigations. He can give me much information about old Jonas and perhaps not a little about this Murat affair, too. So, Peggy, do you think it worthwhile? The captain knows a great deal about you, anyway, and what I want to tell him you can be sure will go no further. How about it?"

There was that about the doctor which inspired absolute trust. All Peggy's arguments to the contrary seemed to go down before his undeniable logic and the kindliness of his intentions.

"All right, Dr. Scott," she conceded. "You can tell Captain Wareham if you like. I don't mind."

"You won't regret it, I think," he answered. "And thank you, Peggy, for allowing me to do so."

CHAPTER XIX

The Captain Joins the Trio

D R. SCOTT'S TALK with Captain Wareham that night was not particularly fruitful of results—so the doctor reported to the girls next morning. The old captain was not surprised to learn that there was some mystery in regard to Peggy's origin. He had always suspected there was something—so he said—but had never supposed it to be quite as far-reaching as it now seemed to be. He had himself, in the past, frequently noticed Peggy digging at the foot of the figurehead but supposed her occupation to be merely some childish diversion. He thought it entirely likely that Olaf had noticed it, too, and furthermore had seen the doctor at the same mysterious work and had thus scented something worth investigating.

The captain added that Olaf had been acting rather peculiarly of late, slinking off by himself at odd times and exhibiting a tendency to roam around on the beach late at night when all others were glad to get to bed. He intended to keep a strict eye on Olaf after this and would at once report to the doctor any further eccentricities of the big Swede.

Concerning Thomas Gilchrist, the one-time Number Three Surfman, he had but one other item of interest to add to what they already knew. He clearly recalled that, several times during the early morning after the night of the fateful storm when the surfman had been injured, Gilchrist had approached him in a singular manner, as if he had something special to say, and had then seemed to change his mind and turned away again. He acted so clearly as if he had something on his mind that the captain finally demanded of him if anything were the matter. Gilchrist hesitated, seemed about to say something, and finally turned it off by complaining that he had a bad headache. The captain told him to take the day off, in consideration of what had happened the night before, and get over it. Gilchrist did so, and that was the last the captain ever saw of him alive.

At the time, the captain thought the man was only hesitating about telling him a little more concerning his physical condition. But now he thought it entirely likely that Gilchrist had been trying to make up his mind to confide in him what he knew about the child he had rescued, and hadn't been able to decide. Probably even then his brain was growing confused and unreliable. It was unfortunate that he hadn't been able to say something that would give a clue.

"But what about Jonas Tow... and the mystery ship... and Prince Murat... and all the rest?" demanded Merwin.

"I asked the captain if he had ever heard of *La Belle Denise* of Marseilles, but he hadn't. He said she was undoubtedly some French ship that had just come over here for the first voyage to these parts. He said it was always suspected that Jonas had explored her pretty thoroughly before anyone else got a chance. But no one thought of his having wrenched off and concealed her nameboard; it was always supposed that that had been torn off by the storm.

"The captain says he thinks it is possible that old Jonas may have had that treasure concealed somewhere about his hiding place in the tangle that we explored. Perhaps he didn't trust it even to the trunk—may have used that only as a blind—and buried the real thing under the floor somewhere. And Gilchrist may have thought it safer to leave it there, after all. The captain wants us to make another try down there and wants to be a member of the party when we do. He's keen on this treasure-hunting business!"

"When shall we go?" asked the girls in one breath, all excitement over the prospect.

"Might as well make it this afternoon. This fine weather isn't going to hold much longer, and it would be decidedly difficult to attempt such a thing during a stormy season. Besides that, my stay here is drawing rapidly to a close. I've already had several days over my month, because the coast happened to be clear, and I may be called back any day for some sudden operation. So we'd better make hay while the sun shines. And, too, the captain is planning to see that Olaf doesn't get out alone this afternoon. Surfman Hartley has promised to stick to him like a burr all day because the captain has told Hartley he rather suspects Olaf of being up to something strange and that he needs watching. Hartley doesn't suspect, of course, that it has anything to do with us, but he will keep Olaf from being up to any tricks, I fancy."

They set out on their expedition that afternoon, accompanied by Captain Wareham, who was as keen as a boy over the quest.

It was a mild summer-like day with a quiet, lazy surf, and long, feathery, plume-like clouds scattered over the sky. But the old captain eyed the horizon with distrust and shook his head dubiously when the others commented on the glorious weather.

"It's whooping up for a reg'lar old walloper!" he informed them. "You can't fool *me* on a day like this! Them mares' tails mean business, and even the air tastes like it's goin' to be pretty thick, and right soon, too."

However, the weather being for the moment above reproach, they hurried along rejoicing in it, content to enjoy the sunshine while it lasted. Captain Wareham having assured them that he had seen old Jonas's hut many times and didn't need a look-in on that, they continued on their way to the wreck and the entrance to the secret tunnel through the tangle of undergrowth and rubbish farther on. But they had scarcely left the wreck and started to penetrate the path leading over the dunes when the doctor stopped and bent down to examine something.

"Hello! What's this? I don't like the looks of these very much!" And they all looked down to behold footprints plainly defined, leading straight along the trail they were themselves pursuing.

"Someone's gone in here ahead of us—and just recently, too!" supplemented the captain. "And what's more, they haven't come back, for the footprints are all pointing one way."

"They can't be Olaf's, anyway," added Peggy, "for they aren't nearly big enough."

"That's true," agreed the doctor, "but whoever has gone on must be in there now, and we must be prepared to meet them. You girls let the captain and me go ahead and meet the intruder first. I don't anticipate any trouble, but if there should be signs of any, both of you run back out of the tunnel and wait for us there."

It was with a feeling of suspense that the four began their journey in through old Jonas's tunnel, single file, the doctor ahead, followed by the captain, the two girls bringing up the rear. What they were to meet when they got to the hidden shack, they found it hard to imagine. But what they actually did see when they got there gave them one of the surprises of their expedition.

Directly in the center of the shack stood Jim McCleod. He had moved the remains of the old trunk quite out of the hut and was digging away with a big spade. The floor of the hut—rough boards only cobbled together at best—he had ripped up, and the entire floor space had been dug up to some depth. Jim was startled beyond words to behold these unexpected visitors and stood speechless for a moment, his spade uplifted, his mouth wide open with astonishment.

"Well," grunted the old captain, "so this is where ye be! How come ye didn't invite *us* to this little party?"

But Jim McCleod was never at a disadvantage for long. In an instant, the spade came down, and a broad grin overspread his freckled face.

"You sure got me good and proper, Cap'n and Dr. Scott!" he laughed. "I'd been thinkin' this thing out for a good while and was goin' to give the girls a surprise. We all figured that we'd finished up with this place when we found there wasn't anything in the old trunk, but I kept thinkin' and thinkin' about it, and finally I gave a guess that maybe old Jonas was only tryin' a fool trick with that empty trunk and was trying to make people think that was all there was to it, when really he buried the loot under the floor somewhere where no one'd think of lookin' for it. Of course it was only a guess, and I didn't want to get the girls all excited about it and then they'd be disappointed, so I figured I'd come up here by myself and hunt around and dig up. And if I found anything, I'd leave it there and bring them up to have the fun of finding it. And if I didn't, no harm'd be done. And anyhow, I thought there was no harm in me doin' it by myself since old Jonas wanted me to have the loot."

He stopped there, evidently waiting for the verdict of the party on his action, but the only response he got was from Captain Wareham.

"Well!" the old man sputtered, "*Have* ye found anything?"

"Not a single thing!" declared Jim, ruefully surveying his work. "I guess somebody got ahead of me, 'cause I found the bottom of the trunk broken and somebody's pried up the floorboards underneath.... I been at this job ever since dinner time and I've dug the whole place up two feet or more, and there hasn't a red cent come to light. I was just goin' to give it up when you folks blew in and gave me the surprise of my life!"

"Oh, go ahead and dig deeper!" cried Captain Wareham. "What's *two feet*! If ye're tired Dr. Scott and I'll take a hand and spell ye." It was plain to be seen that the old captain was the most enthusiastic treasure hunter of them all. He grabbed the spade from Jim and began to make the sand fly in all directions, and the others were glad to take refuge in the tunnel, far enough off to be out of range of his implement. And while they were standing there, Peggy informed Jim (who was obviously curious on the subject) that she and Merwin had confided the secret of the treasure to Dr. Scott and the captain, who had decided on a treasure hunt. She did not tell him any of the rest of it yet; nor did the others mention how much wider in range this mystery really was.

When Captain Wareham was winded, Dr. Scott took a turn at the digging, and after a while a depth of three feet had been reached in the small space and still no slightest sign of anything buried had been unearthed. The search began to seem rather hopeless, and the party at last had to acknowledge complete discouragement.

"It's no use keeping it up any longer," declared Dr. Scott. "Nobody—not even old Jonas, I'm pretty sure—would think it necessary to bury anything any deeper than this. I'm afraid we've exhausted the possibilities of this place. I move that we leave it and try to figure out in some other way where Jonas may have hidden his loot."

The captain was loath to give up the hunt, but even he, with all his interest and enthusiasm, could see the uselessness of continuing the search under these conditions.

When the party got out through the tunnel to the beach again, they found a decided change in the weather, even as Captain Wareham had predicted. The wind was coming directly from the northeast, the sky was overcast with heavy gray clouds, and the breakers were beginning to crash in on the beach.

"I told ye so!" the captain commented as the party began the journey back to the hotel. "It's goin' to be a pretty wild night, or I ain't no weather forecaster."

They tramped along the beach, finding it rather heavy going with the high wind directly in their faces. And the new disappointment they had just experienced in the treasure hunt made the girls a trifle despondent and also somewhat unresponsive to Jim's teasing and joking. Before they reached the hotel, it had begun to rain, and by the time they were at last indoors, they were all soaked to the skin. The captain and Jim had hurried on to the station, and the doctor sent the two girls to change into dry clothes at once.

All during the late afternoon and early evening, the storm raged, hourly growing worse. The wind was a hurricane, coming in terrific blasts and shaking the hotel till the windows rattled and the building actually seemed to rock. Billy had a huge fire going in the lobby stove, and they all sat around it, inclined to be somewhat thoughtful and quiet. Every once in so often, Billy would wander over to the window and stare out into the rain-soaked blackness, coming back to shake his head and mutter:

"This is one of them kinds of storms I don't like—these here October hurricanes. If there's any ships out tonight, the Coast Guard'll have something to do, I reckon."

Dr. Scott was on the point of telling Merwin she had better go to bed and not sit up worrying about the storm any longer when the door opened, and in burst Jim McCleod.

"Doctor, can you come up to the station?" he panted. "One of the men's awful bad hurt, 'n Cap'n wants to know if you'll come up."

"Sure thing!" cried the doctor, springing up instantly. "Just wait till I get my slickers on and my surgical case, and I'll be right with you." And he hurried upstairs to prepare for the visit.

"Who is it that's hurt?" demanded Peggy while they were waiting for the doctor to make ready.

"It's the big Swede, Olaf Hansen," said Jim. "I dunno what he's been into, but he's all smashed up. And the funny thing is, he pretty near had a fit when he heard the cap'n was going to send for Dr. Scott!"

CHAPTER XX

The Night of the Storm

IT SEEMED TO Merwin afterward that she would never in all her life forget that terrible night. She felt that she ought to go to bed; yet she knew that if she did, she would probably lie awake, nervous and worried. So Billy and Mrs. Tate took the responsibility of allowing her to remain with them and Peggy down by the stove, and there they all sat, trying to read or talk, but in reality listening to the storm, wondering when the doctor would be back and whether the hurricane that was raging would leave them with a roof over their heads.

Hour after hour dragged on, and still the doctor did not come. Billy spent the time in speculating on what might have happened to big Olaf and deploring the fact that Jim had not had time to explain more about it. The girls were each privately wondering whether Olaf's accident had any bearing on their own affairs, but they had no chance to share their speculations with each other. At last, after midnight, Jim again burst in upon them, the rain streaming from his slickers in rivulets.

"The doctor says not to wait up for him," he panted. "It was my patrol down the beach, so I said I'd stop in on my way and tell you. Olaf's too bad hurt to leave tonight, and Doc's got to stay with him. He says not to worry. Oh! I wish I could stay by this nice warm fire, but I gotta be on my way. So long!"

"But, hey, Jim!" cried Billy as the boy turned toward the door. "You ain't going before you tell us what's the matter with Olaf, are ye? We're all plum crazy to hear about it."

"Well, I ain't got a minute," hesitated Jim. "I'm on patrol, you know. None of us know just what happened—'cept Bill Hartley, and he won't open his head. Cap'n's orders, he says. All we know is that Bill come in tonight, 'bout sundown, leadin' Olaf, or rather *draggin'* him in, an' the Swede was all busted up—face bleedin', arm hangin' loose, chest smashed in, and I dunno whatnot. Bill wouldn't say a word what happened 'cept to the cap'n, and when Olaf heard we was sendin' for Doc Scott, he let out a yell and said he wouldn't have him, but the cap'n didn't pay any attention to that. That's all I know about it, 'cept that the doctor and the cap'n are in there with him, having a great meeting, and won't let any of the rest of us in. . . . I just got to beat it now. So long!"

The night wore on, and in spite of their fears and their curiosity, a great drowsiness at last overtook the little group around the stove, and they decided to go to bed. The storm had abated somewhat, at least in respect to the violence of the wind, and Billy no longer feared for the safety of the hotel. The driving sheets of rain continued to descend, and Merwin at last sank to sleep listening to the vicious slap of it against her windows. She awoke at an early hour in the morning to find her father bending over her. He had evidently just come in from the station.

"What is it, Dad?" she cried. "I . . . I was so worried about you before Jim came, and then I nearly went crazy to hear what it was all about."

"It's all right," he reassured her. "I was just a little anxious about you because Billy said you were up very late and you were all worrying about the storm, so I came to see how you were before I turned in. Something very interesting has happened. I can't tell you about it now because I'm nearly dead for sleep. But later on in the day, I'll tell you the big piece of news I have for you and Peggy. Now, go to sleep for a while. Billy says he won't have breakfast for us all till late, as we all need sleep."

But there was no more sleep for Merwin after that. She lay there dutifully for an hour or so and then got up, knocked at Peggy's door, and crept into bed with her, where she related in a whisper all that the doctor had said when he came in.

"What do you suppose the big piece of news can be, Peg?" she said. "He acts just as if he had the answer to the whole riddle."

"Oh, I don't know! I hardly dare to think!" shivered the other girl. "I do believe I dread to have it all cleared up 'most as much as I do *not* to. I'm afraid it may mean something unpleasant, some awful change for me."

"Well, he didn't act as if it were anything awful or unpleasant, so I wouldn't worry about that," Merwin reassured her. And straightway they began to count the minutes and hours till the time when the doctor should enlighten them. The time was even longer than they had thought it would be, as he did not wake for breakfast but slept right through to dinner time while the two girls fumed and fretted down in the lobby by the fire. The storm continued, and Billy predicted that it was a three- or four-day nor'easter at the very least. But at last the doctor, sleepy-eyed and yawning, strolled down to join the group around the stove.

"After dinner!" he whispered in answer to Merwin's frantic signal, "When?" And another almost intolerable period of suspense ensued for the girls. But at last the meal was over, and Dr. Scott told Merwin to bring Peggy and come to his room, and he'd let them into the great secret at last.

"I'll tell you first what happened to Olaf," he began when they were gathered there. "You remember the captain said he had commissioned Bill Hartley to keep his eye on Olaf all afternoon and see that he didn't get into any mischief. Well, Bill was a capital sleuth. He said Olaf acted from the first as if he were determined to give him the slip and get off by himself. Bill had proposed that they go fishing down on the bay, but Olaf didn't see that at all and told Bill in so many words that he had his own affairs to attend to. Seeing he couldn't openly hang around with him very well after that, Bill decided to let him go his own way and to do a little quiet trailing, keeping well out of Olaf's range of vision.

"According to Bill's account, Olaf pursued a rather erratic course all afternoon. At first he hung around the old figurehead for a long while in an undecided manner. He'd keep peeking out from the back of it every once in a while and staring up and down the beach as if he were afraid he was being watched. Then he appeared to go off on another tack and started out down the beach, keeping to the other side of the dunes and pretty well out of sight. Bill followed him, also keeping out of sight, but finally lost track of him in a stretch of particularly thick scrub cedar growth a couple of miles down. Said he got up behind a dune, finally, and watched and watched for Olaf to appear out of the southern end of it, but the time passed and Olaf didn't materialize.

"Bill was considerably worried then, fearing that Olaf had given him the slip and would be up to some mischief. Added to that, the weather had changed: it was growing dark and beginning to rain. So he finally decided to abandon all caution about keeping out of sight and boldly go ahead with his search, which he did. It was a long time before he came on Olaf's trail, but at last he found traces of those unmistakable big footprints that the rain had not yet obliterated. And they led him, eventually, straight to the half-ruined hut of old Jonas Tow. Before he even reached it, he heard groans and grunts and half-smothered cries, and when he did reach the place, he found Olaf in a fine fix. The Swede had evidently been poking around in the lean-to part that was half fallen in, you know. He had pulled away a portion of the old bedstead, and that, combined with the heavy wind that had risen, had caused the whole thing to come crashing down on top of him, pinning him under the entire weight of it. He had been in this predicament more than an hour when Bill finally found him.

"Well, Bill said he had the most awful time trying to get Olaf out of there. He was frightfully hurt, and every move that was made caused him agony. But it was even worse when it came to getting him back to the station. The man's arm was broken, he had a bad scalp wound, and, worst of all, the beam had crushed his chest in and he could breathe only with the greatest difficulty. Bill wanted to hurry back and get help, but Olaf insisted that he could make it without any aid besides Bill's, so they tried it. But Bill said it was the most horrible journey he'd ever made. Only Olaf's naturally cast-iron constitution and his immense physical strength enabled him to stand it.

"Then they sent for me. By the time I got there, Olaf was unconscious, and I had a night's work getting him patched up. At first I thought his case was hopeless, he was so done in, but as he seems to have the constitution of an ox, I guess he'll pull through. He was scared pretty stiff about his own condition—thought he was going to die and all that—when he came to and said he wanted to make a confession to me about something. I said to him:

"'You aren't going to die, Olaf, but if you've got something on your conscience—and I'm pretty sure you have—you had better out with it, for it's not going to help your recovery to keep it there.' It wasn't till toward morning that he told me this, after I'd been working over him all night, and I think it was only his feeling of gratitude that thawed him out; if it hadn't been for that, he'd probably have kept the secret. So, by slow degrees— for breathing is horribly difficult for him—he told me how he'd been watching us all around that figurehead lately, and especially the afternoon that you girls told me about what you'd discovered and we dug down and got out the box.

"That roused his curiosity, and late that evening, when no one was about, he went to the figurehead himself and dug around till he found that opening, through which he thrust his hand and arm. His arm is exceedingly long, and he has a reach that few men I've ever seen could boast. He says he felt all around but could discover nothing there, till finally, as far over in a corner as he could reach, his fingers encountered something and he pulled it out. Then he covered up his tracks and went back to the station.

"If you remember, I myself had reached in there that day, as far as I could, and had felt around in every direction without success. But then, I haven't an arm like Olaf's! But to go on: When he got back to the station and had a chance alone, he examined his find, which proved to be a long letter wrapped up in many folds of tarpaulin. What he found in that letter put him on to the fact that there was a valuable treasure hidden somewhere about and started him on the business of sleuthing to find the thing. That he was crossing our trail on the same search, he felt certain, though how we had stumbled on the secret, he couldn't quite figure. But he hoped to beat us to it in finding the loot and then decamp as quickly and quietly as possible from the service of this station.

"Such was his laudable ambition up to last night! He had seen us day before yesterday, doing our extensive digging under the figurehead, and realized that it was rather useless to pursue the quest any further there. Either we had found the treasure—in which case he thought some news of it would have gotten about—or, more likely, we hadn't and were going to give the search up as hopeless. As something in the letter had put him on to the fact that Jonas Tow was mixed up in it, he decided to search the old man's hut yesterday—and did so with the results we know. This was all his story. He begged me to forgive him if he'd interfered with us in any way and also not to tell the captain.

"I told him that the captain already knew all about the affair and that his only course was to make a clean breast of it to the captain also, or allow me to do it for him. And, besides that, he was to give up the letter if he wanted to have the matter overlooked. He agreed to both proposals and directed me where to look for the letter in his dunnage. So here it is!"

From his bureau drawer, the doctor took a packet wrapped in old tarpaulin and laid it in Peggy's lap.

"But what is it?" cried the girls in unison.

"Examine it for yourselves," he answered. "You can

easily read it, for it was written by someone whose handwriting is like copperplate. And while you're doing so, I'll take a run up to the station and have another look at Olaf. He's going to be in a bad way for some time to come."

"But does it explain everything?" they demanded, unfolding the tarpaulin.

"It explains so much that there's only one question left to ask!" answered the doctor, with a twinkle in his brown eyes, as he left them.

CHAPTER XXI

Peggy Learns the Truth

WHEN PEGGY AND Merwin had opened the folds of tarpaulin, several closely written sheets of paper were disclosed, and the girls at once recognized the handwriting as the same as that in the letter found in the old work box. The paper was yellowed and somewhat water-stained, but the fine and beautiful writing was still perfectly legible. Peggy handed the whole thing over to Merwin.

"You read it aloud to me," she said. "I'm so nervous I just can't make it out." So Merwin took the sheets and began to read from them, Peggy sitting with hands clasped in her lap so tightly that the knuckles showed white. This was the only way in which her nervousness was apparent as Merwin began to read:

"'To Whom It May Concern:

"'I, Thomas Gilchrist, Number Three Surfman at this Coast Guard station, wish to make the following statement:

PEGGY LEARNS THE TRUTH

"'I feel that I have sustained a serious injury which, at the very least, may affect my mind in some way. Already my brain seems to be playing strange tricks. I seem to forget for many minutes on a stretch who I am or where I am, and in other ways my thinking becomes confused. So I shall write this statement and hand it to Captain Wareham to keep on file in case anything should happen to me.

"'That child that I brought in from the wreck last night has a strange history which I shall endeavor to give in as few words as possible. Also, she has a rich inheritance of which I am, at the present time, sole guardian.

"'Her name is Margaret Roswell Thayer, and her mother, who bore the same name, her sole surviving near relative, perished last night on the wrecked vessel. The father, Stanton Thayer, died four months ago in Puerto Rico of typhoid fever. It is through the mother, however, that the child's curious history is traced.

"'The mother's grandfather, David Roswell, was as a boy attached to the household of Prince Lucien Murat of Bordentown, New Jersey, in the days when he and his uncle, Joseph Bonaparte, resided there. The boy David, then a young lad in his teens, was a great favorite of Prince Murat's and used to accompany him on all his hunting expeditions. At one time he saved the prince's life when that nobleman would have perished, sinking in a marsh or quicksand down in these very parts.

"'The prince was deeply appreciative of what the lad had done. Being naturally of a very open-hand and generous disposition, he told David that he wished to show his gratitude in some material way, but that he had little of value over here in this part of the world to bestow on anyone. He said, however, that he had a collection of jewels of considerable value buried in a certain spot in Switzerland, where they had been hidden when he fled to America. These had been a gift to him from his uncle, Joseph Bonaparte, at the time of the downfall of Napoleon and had been hidden there for safety till he should find a settled home over here.

"'Joseph Bonaparte himself had had much valuable treasure buried in Europe in various places, but had recovered it since or left the rest to remain hidden till he should go back to Europe. Prince Murat said, however, that he himself never intended to go back and had no one over there whom he could trust to get it. Nor did he especially care, himself, whether or not he ever recovered it as he enjoyed and preferred the simple life he was leading here.

"'He therefore bestowed the treasure on David and gave him explicit directions for finding it. David had no opportunity to avail himself of this privilege till he was a man in middle life, when chance opened for him the way to go to Europe on a matter of business. Leaving his wife and son in Bordentown, he sailed for France and, while there, got to Switzerland, located the treasure, and planned to bring it back with him on a sailing vessel—*La Belle Denise*—some three weeks later. All this was known through a letter to his wife, dispatched immediately after he found the treasure.

"'*La Belle Denise* left Marseilles at the appointed date but was never heard of afterward, and it was supposed that she went to the bottom in some terrible storm with all on board.

"'The wife did not long survive the shock of losing her husband in this tragic way, as she was somewhat of an invalid at the time. But the son, another David Roswell, then a young man of nineteen, grew up and prospered and finally became a wealthy lumber merchant. He lost his wife in the second year after his marriage and was left with a baby daughter, Margaret. I was this David Roswell's confidential agent and secretary, and my wife brought up and helped to educate the little girl till Margaret was about fifteen. In that year, David Roswell, through an ill-advised investment, lost all his money, his business went to pieces, and an attack of pneumonia carried him off in a few days, leaving the girl a penniless orphan with no one to care for her but my wife and myself.

"'We had by that time grown too fond of her to give her up, so we took her into our simple home and she lived with us for five or six years, a very different life from the one of luxury to which she had been accustomed. When she was twenty, she began to teach school near Bordentown.

"'A series of personal misfortunes then caused a change in my own mode of life. I lost my wife in a railroad accident at this time, and the shock of her death, combined with a nervous breakdown, made it necessary for me to seek some different occupation than the desk and clerical work I had always been engaged in. My physician advised a prolonged stay at the seacoast and an occupation out of doors in that region, if possible.

"'Margaret had by that time become engaged to a young fellow, Stanton Thayer, rather against my wishes. The young man was a nice enough chap, but he had his way still to make in the world and was, at the time, only a very poorly paid clerk. But he had accepted a position in a company that wished to send him for an indefinite period to their office in Puerto Rico, and Margaret preferred to go with him rather than to wait till his fortune was made. So she was married and left for Puerto Rico, and I was free to follow out my doctor's orders.

"'I came over to the coast and finally, in the Coast Guard station in this region, I found a permanent berth. Previous to that, I had tried the life at a station on the Long Island coast, at the suggestion of a friend, but did not care for the captain and men there and drifted back to the Jersey shore.

"'I had not been here very long when, in looking over the captain's collection of curiosities one day, I was startled beyond words to come across a little volume of La Fontaine's fables with an inscription on the flyleaf which showed the book was a gift from Prince Murat to one "David R."—surely no other than David Roswell, to whom the treasure had been left! I had heard from my former employer the story of the lost treasure and had always supposed, with him, that the jewels had gone to the bottom in mid-ocean, but here was something that made me doubt that such was the case. How this little relic had come to be in the captain's possession, I could not imagine, but, questioning him about it, I learned of the wreck on this coast of an unknown ship in which, as a boy, he had found the thing.

"'Though I said nothing about it to anyone, the possibility occurred to me that this ship might have been *La Belle Denise* and that old Jonas Tow, who was still alive, though then very feeble, might know something about the wreck—possibly had even found the treasure. I wrote something to this effect to Margaret in Puerto Rico, but she only sent back a joking and skeptical answer. But from other remarks in her letter, I gathered that her life in Puerto Rico was something of a struggle against poverty, and it strengthened me in my determination to run the matter to earth if possible.

"'I then began a systematic pursuit of all espionage on old Jonas and, through circumstances too long to be detailed here, became satisfied at length that he knew much about it. So one day I boldly asked him about *La Belle Denise* and described the mystery ship to him. The effect was astonishing. He broke down and confessed that he had torn off and destroyed the name boards, but that that was all he had done. That he had found anything of value in her he denied absolutely.

"'But the next night when I was off duty, I went to his shack again and found him in bed and plainly very ill. I wanted to get help for him, but he begged me not to go. He said he knew he was dying and didn't want to be left alone. I said that, before he died, he had better tell me that he had found that treasure, and he finally confessed that he had concealed it in a secret hiding place he had and directed me where to find it. He tried to excuse himself by declaring he had been keeping it for his little great-grandson over in Toms River. He died while I was still with him, and I went back and reported the fact at the station. Next day I went and found the jewels just where he said he had hidden them.

"'All this pursuit and detection of Jonas had taken a number of months, however, and in the meantime Margaret had been having a little tragedy of her own. A little daughter had been born to her, but only two months after the baby's arrival, her young husband was stricken with a violent form of typhoid fever and died, leaving her alone with the child. I had advised her to leave and come north immediately, but she answered that she was staying with some people who had been very kind to her and wished her to remain with them, which she had decided it was best to do till the baby was a little older and better able to stand the sea voyage. Added to that, she had very little money and could not afford to make the expensive trip as yet.

"'From that time on, I sent her about all I could spare from my income, but her own ill health and necessities for the baby absorbed the greater part of this. That was before I had definitely located the treasure. After I found it, I felt that she could not get back too soon. And, as money was still scarce, and as I hesitated to raise any on the jewels till Margaret's ownership had been properly established, I wrote telling her that I would make arrangements for her to take passage on a schooner, the captain of which was a friend of mine in whose way I had thrown considerable business when I had been in the employ of Margaret's father. After some correspondence, he agreed to take her and the baby on his next trip to New York, and even to put them off in the region of Barnegat so that they would be spared the tedious trip down from New York. And so they sailed on the ill-fated vessel.

"'Oh, if I had only not given this advice! I feel . . . my head is growing confused again . . . I do not remember what I wrote last . . .'"

"Goodness!" cried Merwin at this point. "It's getting terribly confused, and the writing scrawls all over. I can hardly make out a thing." Peggy said nothing to this but only waited for her to go on.

"There are some words I can't make out," continued Merwin, "and then he goes on:

"'. . . and now I beg of Captain Wareham or anyone into whose hands this may fall . . .' And then there's more scrawling that doesn't make sense. The poor man must have begun to feel awfully ill." She turned from that sheet to the next and last one, remarking as she did so that there was nothing else on that sheet she could decipher. Then she jumped up and with startled eyes faced Peggy.

"There's only one sentence, or part of a sentence, on this sheet," she gasped, "and here it is:

"'. . . and I must now tell where I have concealed the treasure which I brought from Jonas's hiding place. It is . . .'"

"And there's absolutely nothing else!" she ended.

CHAPTER XXII

The Doctor Has an Inspiration

"WELL, WHAT DO you make of it?" Dr. Scott asked of the two girls when he came back a little later from the station.

Peggy was still speechless over the revelation, but Merwin was bursting with questions.

"Tell us what *you* make of it, Daddy," she demanded. "That'll be more to the point. I've got about a million questions to ask and don't know where to begin!"

"One thing, anyway, is settled beyond a doubt," began the doctor, "and that is the question of Peggy's ancestry. I was on the wrong track when I surmised that she might herself be some descendant of the Bonapartes or Murats, but it was a natural surmise, considering the circumstances. Though I did not say so at the time, I rather feared that if she were so proved, there might be some effort made to claim her, even in spite of her adoption by the Tates. And I wasn't sure just what the adoption laws for this state are or how much hold the Tates could claim on her.

"But as it is, I believe from Thomas Gilchrist's account that she has no near relatives left on her mother's side. And as he mentioned nothing about the father's, I take it that probably there are none very near there, either, or they would doubtless have made some effort to do something for her after her father's death. As no one did so, it is pretty certain that there were no close relatives. We'll look into all that later, but meanwhile, Peggy, you can set your heart at rest, for your Grandfather and Grandmother Tate won't be called upon to give you up."

Then, for the first time, Peggy's tense attitude relaxed while a relieved expression crept into her gray eyes.

"Oh, I am glad!" she murmured. "I . . . I was so afraid!"

"But, Daddy," broke in Merwin, "there are so many things about all this that I can't understand. For instance, how did Thomas Gilchrist know that the schooner that came along that day was the one his friends were on? That has always puzzled me."

"There are always going to be a great many unanswered questions about this affair," answered Dr. Scott. "The principal actors in it are all gone now and have left many loose ends in the mystery. Some of the things we can only guess at. As to how he knew the schooner: he had probably been watching for it for days, perhaps even a couple of weeks. If you remember, Dr. Trenway spoke of having seen him that very afternoon, searching the horizon with marine glasses. Undoubtedly he had been doing that right along, only no one had happened to notice, or else didn't think anything of it if they did.

"Gilchrist says that he had made arrangements to have the two passengers put ashore near here. That is a rather unusual proceeding and would be a decidedly dangerous one except in mild weather and down farther toward Barnegat Light, where they could row into an inlet. Perhaps he expected to have some message from the station down below the Light when that happened. But he knew the schooner, all right, when it came along that day—may have had some code arranged with the captain of it to identify it—and he knew besides that there was trouble brewing for it and that it had been impossible to land its passengers down below.

"If only the poor fellow had not been so ill when he tried to write out this statement, he might have been able to explain a great many more of these doubtful points. You can see, from the way the thing ends, that his mind had gone almost completely off before he finished."

"But what do you think happened?" cried Merwin. "And why is it that, though he said in the beginning that he was going to give this to the captain, he never did, but put it in the strange place we found it?"

"A person whose mind is being affected in that way," explained the doctor, "is likely to be responsible only in streaks. He felt that something was wrong—he says that himself—and decided to write the thing out and hand it to the captain before he lost hold of himself. But he never got to that point. He may have thought he had finished it, may even have thought he had given it to the captain. Then another blank fit would overtake him. My own theory is that in one of these periods, he got to wandering around on the beach with the letter and the box still in his possession. He probably got to the region of the figurehead and had a return to clear thinking, but realized that the end was near and that he couldn't get back to the station and so dug a place under the figurehead and shoved the precious things in there, as that appealed to him as the only place of safety for them. You remember they say he was found close by.

"I have been wondering, also, why it was that the box was near enough to that opening to be reached even by Peggy, but the package with the letter was so far away that it took Olaf's long reach to get hold of it. But, as I explain it, he probably threw them both in together and the box, being heavier, landed nearer to the opening. The light package went into a far corner. That is why Peggy did not find it when she found the box.

"Then, too," the doctor went on, "I've wondered why, if he intended to give the letter to the captain, it should have been so carefully wrapped in tarpaulin, as if he intended, after all, to hide it away somewhere where it would need protection. But I talked that point over with Captain Wareham this morning, and we think we have the explanation. The captain says he remembers it was still raining that next morning, and Gilchrist wore his slickers when he went out. It was clear when they found him that evening, but his coat was off and a sleeve and part of the front of it all torn up. They rather wondered at the time how it had been done. Doubtless he realized, when he decided to hide the things under the figurehead, that the letter would need some protection and tore up his coat for a wrapping. He might have undone the work box and put it in with that, but perhaps he did not think of it or decided against it for some reason unknown to us."

It all seemed very plain to them now, and the two girls sat quiet for a moment, thinking it over.

"But, Daddy," Merwin suddenly broke out, "do you realize that, with all this explanation, we're as far as ever from knowing where the treasure is?"

"I was wondering when that was going to dawn on you," he grinned. "Yes, poor Gilchrist was just about to tell when he lost his grip on things completely. Possibly he thought, in his muddled condition, that he *had* explained it. Who can tell? But the sure thing is that we're just as far from that explanation as ever!"

"But shall we keep on hunting for it?" demanded Merwin.

"Indeed we are going to keep on hunting for it!" laughed Dr. Scott. "Only, I confess that I'm somewhat at a loss where to begin now; or, rather, where to continue. We had exhausted the best possibilities before this latest development. I'm not sure just where to begin next. This letter of Gilchrist's has rather unsettled some of my ideas. However, we'll think out something new soon. We're going to find that thing if we have to comb the whole beach from here to the Light to get at it. The captain's as keen on it as the rest of us."

THE DOCTOR HAS AN INSPIRATION

"There's one thing I've been wondering about," said Peggy, and it was the first contribution she had made to the discussion. "I wanted to ask you, Dr. Scott, about that opening in the boards down under the sand in the support of the figurehead. Do you think it was there all the time, or did Thomas Gilchrist make it the day he hid the things under there? If he made it that day, he would have had to do it with a saw or a hatchet, wouldn't he? And I should think he must have been too sick to do that; and, anyway, he would have had to bring those things with him, and there weren't any found around. And if he didn't make the opening, how did he know it was there? He couldn't have hidden the things under the platform unless there'd been an opening of *some* kind, could he?"

The doctor made no reply to this but sat silent for two or three minutes, chin in hand, thinking deeply. Suddenly he sprang up with a smothered exclamation that sounded like, "Thunder in the winter!" and grabbed his slicker coat and sou'wester.

"Peggy, you've got us all licked a mile at this detective business!" he exclaimed. "You've asked the one question that holds the key to the whole puzzle."

"But wait! Wait! Where are you going?" demanded Merwin as he disappeared out at the door.

"I'll answer Peggy's question when I get back!" he called over his shoulder and vanished down the stairs.

"Well! This is *too* much!" cried Merwin, exasperated by the turn affairs had taken and absolutely unable to contain her curiosity another moment. "Anyhow, he didn't say not to follow him, so I'm going to. It isn't storming so very hard now. Get on your slicker, Peggy, while I get on mine, and we'll go see what he's doing."

And three minutes later, the girls were scampering along the wet dunes after the doctor's tall, slicker-clad figure.

CHAPTER XXIII

The Answer to the Riddle

IN SPITE OF her absorption in the affairs of the moment, Merwin gave a little gasp of wondering admiration at the sight of the ocean when she and Peggy reached the top of the dune. As far out as the eye could see, mountainous gray-green and white combers were racing in, breaking on the beach with a continuous thunder. At every crash the foam, whipping to the consistency of clotted cream, was borne clear to the foot of the dunes. Great masses of this foam, freed by the wind, were being tossed hither and yon over the very top of the dunes themselves. Low gray clouds scudded across the sky, spray and sand lashed the girls' faces, and the brine-laden wind whipped their clothes about them at every step and made walking very difficult.

"Wherever is Daddy going?" panted Merwin as they struggled along.

"To the figurehead, of course," answered Peggy, calling it

back over her shoulder. "Where else could it be? Look! He has the spade with him. I wonder what he's going to do!"

They were not to be left long in doubt. They caught up with him just about as he reached the figurehead, almost expecting that he would send them right back. But he did not. Instead, he only shouted above the roar of the wind:

"Stand back out of range. Get into some sheltered spot, if you can, and don't interrupt me till I've opened the way into this place again!"

The girls crouched down in the lee of one of the dunes, wondering if the doctor had suddenly gone crazy, and watched while he hurled great spadefuls of wet sand down behind him. Being damp clear through, the sand was much easier to handle and quicker to dispose of than it had been in its dry state. After a while the planks left after the first digging began to be visible.

"Whatever do you suppose he's digging there for again?" marveled Merwin. "We exhausted all the possibilities of that place the other day."

"He must have some good reason," declared Peggy confidently. "Perhaps he only wants to see that opening again. He may find out something from that."

A little later they heard a voice calling, "Ahoy, there!" and, looking back toward the hotel, saw old Captain Wareham striding up to them along the dune, amazement written large all over his face.

"Has the doctor gone crazy?—or have you all?" he exclaimed as he came up to them. "What's all this mean, anyhow? I saw ye from the lookout and had to come right down and find out!"

"I don't blame you for thinking we're crazy!" laughed Merwin. "We don't know what Dad is after ourselves. You'd better go and ask him."

The captain went over and had a short interview with Dr. Scott but apparently got as little satisfaction as the girls had, for the doctor was plainly in no mood to explain things just at that moment. Then the captain took the shovel and dug for a spell while the doctor rested. After what seemed an age, the opening into the figurehead's support was again laid bare, and the girls crowded up to see what was going to happen next.

They were soon to know. Taking his big electric torch from a pocket, the doctor crawled down into the tunnel and wedged himself through the opening. And the captain, though of a much stouter build, managed in some incomprehensible manner to do the same. The two girls, totally unable now to keep so far away, also clambered down into the tunnel but were sent back peremptorily by the doctor.

"Don't try to get down here!" he shouted. "You'll have the whole thing caving in on us, and then you'll have to dig us out. We'll be out in a few minutes, and then you'll know all about it."

It seemed to Merwin and Peggy a far longer time than "a few minutes" as they stood off at a little distance, uneasily watching the opening. By this time their clothes and hair were soaked with salt spray in spite of the protection of their slickers, their lips tasted salty, and their very eyes and nostrils stung with the brine. But little they cared, so deeply were their minds concentrated on what was going forward.

Merwin had just started to remark, "Well, I can't see what..." when they heard a shout from the interior, and a moment later the doctor struggled out, dragging after him something the nature of which they could not guess. How the old captain got out, they never stopped to see, for the doctor called to them to come and help him lift something out of the trench and then get back as fast as they could to the hotel.

"Don't talk to me just yet!" he panted. "I'm rather winded, and we're all soaked to the skin and must get into dry things at once. We've found it, that's all! Here it is, in this metal chest. The captain and I will bring it along. You two go on and get your clothes changed, and we'll have all the explanations later."

Somehow or other the girls got back and into dry things, and after what seemed to them an eternity of needless delays, the doctor called them into his room and exhibited a strange old flat metal box or chest, some eight inches high and about a foot long, standing on his table.

"There it is!" he said.

"But what's in it?" they both cried, forgetting for the moment all other questions in this one paramount query.

"Open it and see!" he answered.

They tiptoed over to it as cautiously as if it were charged with dynamite and lifted the lid. And there before them lay a strange and breath-taking assortment of articles.

The two girls fingered the rich contents gingerly. Here were broken sword handles crusted with gems, broken sections of jeweled crowns or tiaras, frayed ribbons with jeweled clasps or fastenings, cameo brooches and filigree eardrops, all jumbled together, as if they had been hastily gathered up before some wild flight by someone who only cared to take them all to a place of safety and thought little of their condition or number so long as they were got out of sight.

"How very strange!" breathed Merwin at last. "And these belonged to the Bonapartes at one time—some perhaps even to Napoleon! And think what they've been through and where they've been since!"

"But how did you find them, Dr. Scott?" asked Peggy, coming back to the main issue. "And how did you know they were there?"

"It was your question, Peggy, that suddenly made me suspect the truth," answered the doctor contentedly. "You struck the nail right on the head when you asked how Thomas Gilchrist knew that opening was there when he threw the letter and work box under the platform the day after the wreck. Of course he didn't make that big opening *that* day—it would have been a physical impossibility in the state he was in then—and of course he knew it was there because he'd made it himself at some other time, when he concealed the jewels there that he had brought from old Jonas's hiding place. That occurred to me the minute you asked your question.

"And one other thing occurred to me at the same time. The loot must be in there somewhere, even if it weren't hidden in the sand as we had thought. Therefore there was only one thing to do—get in there again and have another look around. I had an idea where it might be, and, as it proved in the end, I wasn't mistaken. Gilchrist had got in there, perhaps intending to dig in the sand and bury the chest, and then probably had thought better of it because sand is a shifting quantity, anyhow, and the gems might be injured by exposure to dampness. Instead, he sawed out an opening in the wooden platform above his head, found a hollow place in the bottom of the figurehead itself, inserted the chest in that, and replaced the boards. No cleverer or safer hiding place could possibly have been invented. It was absolutely safe from detection, even if anyone had seen him working around the figurehead—which they probably didn't, as no doubt he did the job at night.

"Well," Dr. Scott concluded, "we've solved the riddle. There is the treasure. I've no idea as yet what it's all worth. It will take an expert gem assayer and an antiquity authority to decide that. But I imagine it will be a considerable sum.... And now, Peggy, don't you think it's high time we called your Grandfather and Grandmother Tate and let them into the secret?"

And this time Peggy raised no objection!

On a brilliant moonlit night some four weeks later, three figures stood on the dune close to the figurehead. A cold November wind had whipped the ocean into combers

THE ANSWER TO THE RIDDLE

that crashed down on the beach and broke in sheets of molten silver. The two shorter figures were Merwin and Peggy, huddled in warm wraps; the tall form was that of Dr. Scott. He had just returned to the shore after an absence of nearly a month, having been called back to his office almost immediately after the dramatic find of the treasure.

"I wanted you not to miss this sight," he said to Merwin, "especially as you are to go back with me tomorrow. You've certainly made wonderful progress in regaining your strength, daughter. I shouldn't know you for the pale little sprout I brought down here with me two months ago!"

"But tell us what you've found out about the jewels," demanded Merwin, impatient to hear all the news at once. "Have they decided yet how much they are worth?"

"That's going to take some time," answered the doctor, smiling at her impatience. "The experts think probably the things will bring more sold as antiquities than as separate jewels out of their settings. And they are trying to trace as much as they can of their history. But one thing is certain: Peggy is going to receive a comfortable sum from the sale of them and needn't worry about expenses for some time to come.

"And now I have a proposition to make to you, Peggy. And before I tell you what it is, I want you to know that I have talked it over with Bill and Mrs. Tate and have their full agreement on the matter. We want you to leave the beach here for a while and come to the city with Merwin and me and try going to school with Merwin and getting an education right side by side with her. You can come back here any time you wish if you happen to get lonely and want a glimpse of your grandpa and grandma—and the old figurehead here. How about it, Peg?"

For a moment Peggy was so startled that she could not collect her thoughts sufficiently to reply. Then her first impulse was to cry, "Oh, no, no! I can't leave here, ever!" But Merwin was squeezing her hand and looking at her with such an imploring expression that she could not voice the thought. Then it suddenly came over her that the beach would be a very lonely place when Merwin left it on the morrow, and that the emptiness of her days after that would be almost unendurable. After all, under the doctor's kindly protection and with Merwin's affectionate companionship, she could doubtless be happy, temporarily, without the beach and all it meant to her. Suddenly all her defenses broke down.

"Yes ... oh, thank you both ... so much! I'll come!" she faltered while Merwin hugged her ecstatically.

The doctor only smiled, but there was a pleased expression in his eyes as he assured her:

"That's capital! I think you've made a wise choice, Peggy. And you've certainly pleased everyone by it.... But there's one more thing I want to speak of," he went on. "And that's about Jim McCleod. I think he ought to be told something about how we found the treasure, after all, and in so doing you'll have to give him a little idea of the history about yourself, Peggy, and why the jewels belong to you. I think it's due him in view of old Jonas's wish about it."

"Oh, I've told him all about it already," said Peggy, surprisingly. "I thought he ought to know, too. And, Dr. Scott, there is something else that I'd like to ask your advice about. I feel as if Jim ought to have *something* out of all that treasure, even if it doesn't belong to him. He's such a nice boy, and he was awfully good about keeping our secret when we asked him to. The other day he told me his greatest ambition was to have a motor boat—he's got his eye on a second-hand one right now—and leave the Coast Guard station and set up a crab-and-clam business on the bay. If I could, I think I ought to see that he gets that boat. Do you think we could manage it . . . out of what I get from . . . those jewels?"

"Most certainly we can, and it's very generous of you to think of it, Peggy," replied the doctor. "We'll see that he gets his boat in the shortest record time. But now I think we ought to go in and spend the rest of this last evening with your grandfather and grandmother."

"I shall miss the figurehead!" sighed Merwin as they took one last look at the sea and at the great wooden figure brooding over it. "She's come to mean a whole lot in my life."

"She always *did* mean a lot in mine," responded Peggy softly. "More even than I dreamed!"

One more last, long look they took at the great draped statue with its exultant seaward gaze, then, in silence, turned and walked back over the dunes in the moonlight.

MORE BOOKS FROM THE GOOD AND THE BEAUTIFUL LIBRARY

Flag in Hiding
by Trella Lamson Dick

Rocket Genius
by Charles Spain Verral

Trumper
by Hetty Burlingame Beatty

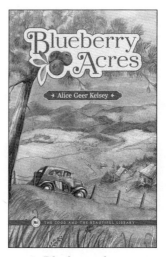

Blueberry Acres
by Alice Geer Kelsey

goodandbeautiful.com